THE
CAPITALIST
SPIRIT

THE
CAPITALIST
SPIRIT

Toward a Religious Ethic
of Wealth Creation

EDITED BY
PETER L. BERGER

ICS PRESS

Institute for Contemporary Studies
San Francisco, California

HB
501
.C24277
1990
154649
Jan.-1992

Inquiries, book orders, and catalog requests should be addressed to ICS Press, Institute for Contemporary Studies, 243 Kearny Street, San Francisco, CA 94108. (415) 981-5353. Fax (415) 986-4878. For book orders and catalog requests call toll free within the United States except Alaska and Hawaii: (800) 326-0263. Distributed to the trade by National Book Network, Lanham, Maryland.

Designed by David Peattie. Indexed by Shirley Kessel.

Library of Congress   Cataloging-in-Publication Data

The Capitalist spirit: toward a religious ethic of wealth creation /
   edited by Peter L. Berger.
      p.   cm.
Includes index.
ISBN 1-55815-112-5 (cloth)
1. Capitalism—Religious aspects. I. Berger, Peter L.
HB501.c24277   1990
330.12'2—dc20   90-42825
                                                           CIP

CONTENTS

FOREWORD

Many believe that the death of communism—from East Germany and Czechoslovakia to the Soviet Union and the third world—means the end of the animus against capitalism. Whereas socialism has proved an abject failure in raising standards of living significantly in the numerous societies in which it has been attempted, capitalism has successfully produced economic growth in a wide variety of cultures around the world. The empirical data would suggest that the great ideological battle of modern times is over.

But man does not live by facts alone. And the socialist vision—a dream that, as Peter L. Berger writes, "haunts the intellectual imagination of the West"—is not unique to our time and place. Its roots can be found in the early Jewish and Christian cultures from which our ethical traditions are derived. Much of socialism's appeal is its image of a truly communitarian society, an image that is by definition premodern and therefore concerned not with the production of wealth but rather with its just distribution. It is an image particularly appealing to modern intellectuals.

Capitalism, through its sheer ability to deliver the goods, has emerged as the most revolutionary force in human history. It has enabled entire societies to produce great wealth for the first time. It is a stunning irony, therefore, that capitalism seems to lack a serious ethical structure to legitimize its unique contribution: the creation of wealth. *The Capitalist Spirit* represents a first attempt to explore the resources for such an ethic. It is an exploration the Institute intends to continue.

Robert B. Hawkins, Jr., President
Institute for Contemporary Studies

INTRODUCTION   PETER L. BERGER

Concern for the poor and, as a result, concern for discrepancies of wealth have been deeply rooted in the Hebrew Bible, in the New Testament, and in both Jewish and Christian ethical thought since the scriptural period. It is an offense to divinely mandated justice that some should go hungry while others are living in luxury, and redress of this discrepancy has been proclaimed as a religious as well as moral duty since the time of the prophets of ancient Israel. Biblical and postbiblical texts are full of warnings against the dangers of wealth for the pious. In recent Roman Catholic thought this central theme of Judeo-Christian ethics has been caught in the phrase "the preferential option for the poor," meaning that it is a religious duty to side with the poor and, beyond this, that the condition of the poor serves as a principal criterion in assessing a society morally.

For the moment there is no need to criticize the debatable theological and political assumptions that have accompanied the phrase among the liberation theologians who first coined it—such as the idea that the struggle for social justice is the core of the Gospel or the notion that Marxist categories are adequate in understanding the contemporary world. If brackets are put around these assumptions (which are, in my opinion, thoroughly misguided), there is no reason to quarrel with the phrase as such. The same phrase, however, leads to a very distorted view of economic realities if wealth is seen as some sort of inert entity, a given, with the only moral problem being its distribution. Except under the most primitive conditions (a subsistence economy in a tropical paradise, for example), wealth is never given—it must be created. Precisely if one affirms a preferential option for the poor, one must ask which "modes of production" (to use Marx's handy term) are most conducive to the mitigation or the eradication of poverty. This question is especially relevant in the highly dynamic circumstances of modern industrial development, which, for the first time in human history, has made explosive economic growth a reality for millions of people.

Put simply, religious thought has had a very hard time dealing with the moral challenge of modern capitalism. The foundations of Jewish and Christian moral sensibilities are premodern; ipso facto they are communalistic, inspired by an imagery of agrarian economies in which a more or less static pie is to be sliced up in an equitable fashion. It is no wonder, then, that so many religious thinkers have been anticapitalist and prosocialist in their instinctive inclinations. Socialist thought, too, despite its modernistic and putatively scientific aspirations, has also been influenced to a remarkable degree by such premodern images of bucolic harmony. Marx himself, I think it can be shown, was torn between contradictory images of modern productivity and premodern communalism. Be this as it may, if one is persuaded on empirical grounds (as, I believe, one has to be) that a preferential option for the poor must make one favor the capitalist over the socialist option, one is faced with very few religious resources for a moral legitimation of this position.

In Christian history there has been one important exception to the neglect of an ethic of production as against an ethic of distribution. This has been not so much Calvinism as such, but rather the post-Calvinist developments in a number of Protestant denominations, especially in the Anglo-Saxon world. These developments, of course, were the topic of Max Weber's work on the relation of Protestantism to the culture of capitalism. I continue to think that Weber's interpretation of this relationship was correct historically and that, more important, it helps to explain a number of important contemporary phenomena (such as the dramatic growth of conservative Protestantism in the third world, especially in Latin America). The same insouciant identification of Christian morality with capitalism can be found on the evangelical right in the United States. All of this is very significant sociologically. For myself (and, I daresay, for most if not all the contributors to this volume), these contemporary reincarnations of the Weberian constellation, whatever their sociological interest, are not any help for theological and ethical reflection. In other words, if one is not persuaded by the theological and ethical doctrines of Jerry Falwell, or those of Guatemalan converts to Pentecostalism, the problem continues to be there.

If the problem is irksome for (let us say) right-of-center academics, it is downright painful, in a very practical way, for religious businesspeople. George Weigel, in his chapter, vividly describes this practical dilemma for a Roman Catholic businessperson in the United States today—a person who likes his work and is successful at it, who is convinced that he is living a morally acceptable life—and who, when he turns to those who speak for his church (bishops as well as theologians), hears nothing but deprecation, if not condemnation, of everything he does and stands for. The same situation can easily be found among Protestant and Jewish businesspeople. If one does indeed believe that capitalist enterprise is a morally legitimate vocation, of great importance for the well-being of society (including the poor), then this situation is unfortunate. It is also serious theologically if a religious community leaves in the lurch, and with a feeling of stigmatization, large numbers of its own members who are trying hard to live honorably by its precepts.

The chapters by Robert Grant and David Novak show in some detail how biblical and postbiblical thought in the Judeo-Christian stream focused on the just distribution of wealth, with little attention paid to its just creation. Both chapters, however, indicate some possibilities of religious resources for an ethic of

3

wealth creation. Michael Novak discusses the revolution in ethical thinking brought about by the Scottish Enlightenment and its implications for thinking about capitalism today. Here is a historically important tradition of moral philosophy that continues to be very relevant today. George Weigel vividly describes the anticapitalist animus in American Roman Catholicism, though he also points to openings toward a different ethical stance. He also describes an interesting sociological paradox: just at the time when Roman Catholics have really made it in American society, there has occurred an ascendancy of anticapitalist and at least implicitly anti-American ideology in the official circles of their church. Weigel has some significant things to say about this concurrent emergence of a Roman Catholic "CEO class" and a Roman Catholic "new class." Walter Block argues forcefully that (*pace* Ayn Rand and some of her followers) a libertarian ethic need not be antireligious. Last but by no means least, Richard J. Neuhaus argues that, contrary to Karl Barth's approach, a Christian view of the economic world should not neglect the element of whimsy—in his words, looking upon economic activity as a "playful participation in creation." Perhaps appropriately, the book ends with Mozart rather than Adam Smith.

It is not suggested that this volume provides a religious ethic of wealth creation; a sustained effort of people in different disciplines and from different traditions will be required to do that. Nevertheless, it is hoped that this preliminary exploration will open avenues of thought for others who have become concerned with the problem. A word about the selection of contributors: they do not exactly constitute a roster of well-known leftists. This is by no means accidental. The purpose of this symposium was not to engage in a debate with the religious Left, an exercise that several of the contributors have engaged in many times. Rather, the purpose was to bring together a group of people, most of whom have broadly similar views on the economic realities, in order to explore the theological and ethical implications of their common position. The papers were discussed at a meeting of the contributors in Washington, D.C., in October 1989, after which a number of revisions were made.

This volume is a project of the Institute for the Study of Economic Culture at Boston University, a center for research on the relations between culture and socioeconomic change. The role of the Institute for Contemporary Studies in the publication of this volume is very much appreciated. The project was funded by the John M. Olin Foundation. I want to express my great appreciation for this support.

ONE

ROBERT M. GRANT

Early Christianity
and the Creation of Capital

In a quest for ethical principles bearing on the creation of capital, we need to consider what Christianity and Judaism have taught on the theme. We run into difficulties, however, when we search the records of Christian beginnings and the formative years of the church. Two thousand years ago not much was being said about capital, especially among Jewish and Christian leaders. The founder of Christianity said next to nothing about anything resembling capital formation. He expected that the reign of God would come soon and told a man who was looking for eternal life that, though he had kept the ten commandments, he lacked one thing. "Go, sell all that you have, and give it to the poor, and you will have treasure in heaven; and come, follow me" (Mark 10:17–22 and parallels). If that is the end of the matter, there is little point for Christians or their churches to consider the creation of wealth. The history of the Christian church shows, however, that the matter did not end there.

None of Jesus' earliest followers seems to have heard of capital formation. The sayings of Jesus show no enthusiasm for or even

7

interest in the accumulation of wealth. His lack of concern was due primarily to his belief that the reign of God was coming immediately or had even begun to arrive; in addition he was concerned with religious attitudes rather than politics or economics. He and his disciples denounced the love of money or riches. Indeed, Jesus once insisted that it was virtually impossible for a rich man to enter into the kingdom of God. It was harder than for a camel to get through a needle's eye, though with God everything was possible (Mark 10:25–27 = Matt. 19:24–26 = Luke 18:25–27). (Later exegetes adjusted this saying by claiming that "camel" meant rope, or that there was a gate in Jerusalem called Needle's Eye through which a camel could pass, or could pass on its knees!) No early Christian was concerned with the problems faced by capitalism or its ancient analogues. Few differentiated capital from income and none understood what depreciation was. In the Roman Empire there was certainly an awareness of the nature of property and the possibility of a return from it, as well as of debt and interest, as we shall see. There was no economic analysis in the ancient world; "economics" simply meant household or estate management, as in Xenophon's *Oeconomicus*. Good management meant making an estate grow. The Roman politician Cicero urged his son to read Xenophon, but he regarded the whole subject as practical, suited for bankers rather than philosophers.[1]

What Is Capital?

Capital in modern economics means an accumulation of means of production that allows human labor to produce more than it could otherwise. Capital is the major instrument of higher labor productivity, higher incomes, and greater human welfare. Obviously it can be accumulated only if people do not consume all they produce, but save part of it—if there is thrift. Neither work nor thrift alone makes capital, for savings can be used for consumption by the poor, or politicians, or religious leaders. What makes savings into capital in the economic sense is the use to which the savings are put, that is, for production. Since early

Christian teaching was not concerned with production or human productivity, it is difficult to find any relation between this teaching and the inchoate ideas about capital that existed in antiquity. There were, however, many Christian views on wealth, conceived as personal riches, independent of any economic functions. These early views were concerned almost entirely with distribution, that is, with fairness.

Relevant Biblical Passages

Despite the absence of direct comments, it may be possible to find traces of guidelines for ethics in what biblical writers imply or take for granted. Such is the case especially in the parables of Jesus, not so much in their basic statements as in what they take for granted in the Palestinian setting, and in some of Paul's passing comments. Depictions of real-life situations may reveal abiding attitudes toward human behavior, including work, the acquisition of property, and even capital formation.

Before we turn to the New Testament, however, we must recall that the Bible of the early church contained the Old Testament as well as the New. Calvin's emphasis on the Hebrew scriptures would not have surprised early Christians, and they would have sought for insights from the beginning of Genesis onward. The creation story raised important questions. Do men have to work because of a curse laid on Adam after he disobeyed God? According to Genesis 3:18 and 3:20, Adam was to eat his bread in sorrow and by the sweat of his face. A sensible exegesis can note that this was not the first mention of his toil. God originally set him in Eden "to till it and guard it" (2:15); thus, according to the biblical story, work was Adam's original destiny, though God insisted again on work when he condemned Adam's disobedience. Later came the division of labor and the rise of civilization, along with keeping sheep, building cities, living in tents and raising cattle, playing musical instruments, and forging with bronze and iron (Gen. 4). Still later, Noah built a very large ship, obviously from his accumulated savings, and after the flood he

9

was able to plant a vineyard. His descendants tried to build the tower of Babel with baked bricks and bitumen mortar. As social life developed, money was used in Abraham's time, or at any rate is mentioned in relation to him. Abraham's son Isaac prospered from his work. He is said to have "sowed . . . and reaped in the same year a hundredfold. The Lord blessed him, and the man became rich, and gained more and more until he became very wealthy. He had possessions of flocks and herds, and a great household, so that the Philistines envied him" (Gen. 26:12–14).

Later Hebrew literature emphasizes the importance of work. The book of Proverbs recommends imitation of the ant, which prepares food for winter in the summer, obviously by forethought and frugality. Human sluggards risk poverty when they indulge in "a little sleep, a little slumber, a little folding of the hands to rest" (Prov. 6:6–11). "The slack hand brings poverty but the diligent hand brings wealth" (10:4). Wealth is better. Another wisdom book, Sirach (Ecclesiasticus), insists that what you need for daily life must be your own, not begged for (Ecclus. 40:28–30). Even earlier, Greek poets were making points like these. In the seventh century Hesiod claimed that "both gods and men are angry with a man who lives idle," and urged that "if your heart within you desires wealth, do these things and work with work upon work"— that is, strenuously.[2] Many relatively timeless Greek proverbs express this view, but it has nothing to do with capital as such.

The Old Testament prophets, like the contemporary Greek reformers, denounced excess and injustice in the acquisition of property, chiefly real estate. Isaiah attacked developers in his day: "Woe to those who join house to house, who add field to field, until there is no more room and you are made to dwell alone in the midst of the land." Agricultural yields were evidently the source of the wealth, for as they decline "many houses shall be desolate, large and beautiful houses, without inhabitant" (Isa. 5:8–10). Jeremiah offered general denunciation, claiming that "from the least to the greatest everyone is greedy for unjust gain" (Jer. 8:10). He attacked the man who "gets riches but not by right" (17:11) or "makes his neighbor serve him for nothing and does not give him his wages" (22:13). He also predicted the capture of Jerusalem and the destruction of the temple by the king of Babylon, and was denounced by the priests and prophets, though supported by the princes and the people. As a sign that the long-term trend was favorable, however, he bought temporarily depressed real estate, for God had said, "Houses and fields and vineyards shall be bought in this land again" (32:9–15). Other prophets denounced profiteering; Ezekiel criticized those who "take interest and increase and gain from their neighbors by extortion" (Ezek. 22:12). More proverbially, Koheleth (Ecclesiastes) noted the limitless urge to accumulate: "He who loves money will not be satisfied with money, nor he who loves wealth, with gain: this also is vanity. When goods increase, they increase who eat them; and what gain has their owner but to see them with his eyes?" (Eccles. 5:10–11). Obviously capital was not being formed under these circumstances. These Old Testament passages show that there was a considerable concern for the creation of wealth among ancient Jews.

The Teaching of Jesus

The teaching of Jesus points to the importance of natural productivity, notably in regard to wheat and grapes, the sources of mankind's daily bread and wine. The parable of the sower tells of seeds producing welcome returns of one hundred, sixty, and thirty times (Mark 4:3–8 and parallels). Several other parables insist on growth—from the smallest seed of the mustard weed to the greatest bush (Mark 4:30–32 and parallels), or from yeast to bread (Matt. 13:33 = Luke 13:20–21). In spite of such expectations and hopes, work remains basic. A parable of Jesus tells how one son refuses to work in his father's vineyard but then does so, while another says he will work but does not. Only the first "did the will of his father," for deeds, not words, are what count (Matt. 21:28–32). Luke criticizes those who offer typical excuses for not working, such as the need to visit a field just bought or to examine oxen recently acquired, or the fact of a recent marriage (Luke 14:18–20; cf. Deut. 20:5–7, 24:5). Wages obviously have a part to play but are discussed only in the parable of the laborers in the vineyard

(Matt. 20:1–15). Early in the morning the owner of a vineyard hired laborers for a denarius a day. Later he went to the marketplace and hired others who were standing idle, for "whatever is right." Even at the eleventh hour he hired more workmen. Presumably the grapes were in danger of becoming overripe and it was necessary to get them picked. At evening he told his steward to pay each man a denarius, and those hired first began to complain. He denied doing them wrong; they had agreed on a denarius, and in any case he could do what he chose with what belonged to him. There is no hint of a minimum wage doctrine here, or of equal pay for equal work. The situation demanded action, for the crop had to be saved. In any case, the decision is the employer's. (The appended moral, "The last will be first and the first last," has nothing to do with the story.) These examples show only what one can do with what one has and do not tell how one can accumulate wealth. Less is said about acquisition than one might expect, but we shall see that early Christians did in fact discuss various trades and professions that could bring profits.

The general situation presupposed is that of moderately prosperous landowners and their employees in early first-century Palestine. Great wealth is rarely mentioned, and there is nothing like the rich and acquisitive society centered in Rome. Those who work engage in carpentry, fishing, and farming. Ancient authors held that such manual laborers ranked below physicians, soldiers, and tax collectors, not to mention the stewards of masters often absent. These authors and their Christian colleagues criticized trading and money changing, and encouraged slaves to work diligently. This was not the environment in which the question of capital formation would arise.

Stewardship and the Acquisition of Wealth

Some of the parables of Jesus deal with stewards; these shed some light on the origin and preservation of wealth. Apparently he was well acquainted with absentee landlordism and problems related to it and for this reason laid strong emphasis on the obligation of stewards to be trustworthy (Luke 16:10 = Matt. 25:21). "He who is trustworthy with very little is trustworthy also with much, and he who is dishonest with very little is dishonest also with much. If you have not been trustworthy with unjust riches, who will entrust genuine riches to you?" Similarly the apostle Paul teaches that "stewards are required to be trustworthy" (1 Cor. 4:2).

A good steward is rewarded by promotion (Matt. 24:45–47 = Luke 12:42–44), but bad stewards will be punished severely. When a master's return is delayed, a wicked slave might beat his fellow slaves and eat and drink with those who get drunk. On his return the master will punish this slave (Matt. 24:48–51 = Luke 12:45–46). Steward-slaves may act inequitably toward either their fellows or their masters. For instance, a slave whose master forgives a debt of ten thousand talents may try to enforce payment of much smaller loans due to himself (Matt. 18:24).[3] In other words, the parable sets forth a situation more likely among rich Romans and oriental kings than among Jesus' immediate circle; but this simply means that it has a point for the world outside. Only Luke (7:41–43) records a rather unrealistic parable about two debtors, one who owed fifty denarii and one who owed five hundred. When they had no assets the moneylender forgave both. The man who owed more, it is supposed, will love the lender more.

In another parable a rich man hears that his steward is wasting his money and asks for the accounts. The steward expects to be dismissed and, since he is too old and feeble for manual labor, tries to ingratiate himself with others by discounting their debts to his master.[4] When the master learns about the steward's actions he "commend[s] the dishonest steward for his prudence; for the sons of this age are more prudent in dealing with their own generation than the sons of light" (Luke 16:1–8). This is one moral. In the course of transmission several more have been added. The first of these shifts from description to counsel about unrighteous riches. "I say to you, Make friends for yourselves by means of unrighteous mammon, so that when it fails they may receive you into the eternal abodes" (16:9). Another provides general counsel about divided loyalties: "No one can be a slave to two masters; either he will hate the one and love the other, or cling to one and despise the other. You cannot be a slave to God and mammon" (16:13). Finally, the parable receives a historical setting. "The Pharisees heard all this and because they loved money they mocked him" (16:14). It looks as if the parable originally conveyed no morals of this kind; the various applications were apparently added from other parts of the tradition, especially by Luke.

The parable of the talents (Matt. 25:14–30) or pounds (Luke 19:12–27) tells of a master who entrusts funds to three slaves in the ratio 5:2:1 ("to each according to his ability" in Matthew's version). Here we finally see capital, working capital at that, and in the process of formation. The most vocal slave is given one unit and buries it. "Master, I knew you are a hard man, reaping where you did not sow and collecting where you did not scatter; in fear I went away and hid your unit in the ground; see, you have what is yours." The master coldly replies that having drawn this conclusion the slave should have invested the funds with bankers so that he might collect the money with interest.⁵ The parable now ends with the rather cryptic moral that "more will be given to him who has, but even what he has will be taken from him who does not have," a conclusion the synoptic evangelists also use elsewhere (Matt. 13:12 = Mark 4:25 = Luke 8:18). Such high rates of return were satirized around this time by the Roman poet—and millionaire—Persius: "Sell your spirit for lucre! Trade, adroitly combing every border of the world. . . . Expand your fortune twofold! Done! Three, fourfold it's coming in—ten times I've increased it. Put me a mark to stop at!"⁶ Two more gospel parables accept the goal of large returns. A man covers up a treasure he has found in a field, then sells all he has and buys the field, obviously relying on "inside information" to take advantage of the previous owner (Matt. 13:44). Similarly, a trader in search of fine pearls finds a precious one and puts all his assets into buying it (Matt. 13:45).

Problems of Inheritance

In the Graeco-Roman world as elsewhere inheritance played an important role. A strange parable perhaps related to the crucifixion of Jesus tells of wicked tenants who refuse to pay rents, harm or kill various collectors sent to them, and finally kill the owner's son in the mistaken belief that the vineyard will then belong to them (Mark 12:1–12 and parallels). The parable assumes a complete breakdown of government.

A more normal picture of inheritance appears in the parable of the rich fool, rich because of his productive land (Luke 12:16–21). He proposes to build bigger barns even though he has "ample goods laid up for many years." The basic criticism seems to be that he lacks moderation and may indeed be blind to human limitations. He is acquisitive. He does not follow the typical advice, given, for example, by the poet Persius: "In money, learn proportion and just desire."[7] Such a point is underlined when God says, "Fool, tonight your life is required of you, and as for the things you have prepared, whose will they be?" (Luke 12:20). This is the proverbial wisdom expressed in Sirach 11:18–19: "There is one who grows rich from his wariness and frugality, and this is the portion of his reward. While he says, 'I found rest and now I will eat of my goods,' he does not know at what time he will pass away and leave them to others and will die."[8]

Another parable related to proverbial wisdom is the story of the prodigal son who asks his father for his half of what he expects to inherit. The father, not heeding the counsel of Sirach 30:19–20, divides his property between his two sons. Sirach had recommended not giving "a son or a daughter, brother or friend, power over yourself during your lifetime. . . . It is better for your children to ask you than for you to look to the hands of your sons."[9] So it turned out. The younger son wasted his half and the older son owned all that was left. When the father gave the returned prodigal "the best robe," a ring and shoes, and killed the fatted calf for him, he was wrongly using the other son's property for his own charitable projects (Luke 15:11–32). Such points are less important than the father's generosity, but they are there.

Though Jesus did not condemn the formation of capital, his message taken as a whole does not encourage it. He told his hearers that they were living in a crisis situation; one such announcement out of many is that of Luke 17:26–27 (= Matt. 24:27–30). In

ancient times ordinary human activities—eating, drinking, mar-
rying, buying, selling, planting, building—were terminated by
flood or fire, and so it will be "in the days of the Son of Man."
Like the Old Testament narratives, the gospel sets limits to human
initiatives and achievements; it relativizes their importance and
directs attention to the power and working of God. Jesus specifically insists on the difficulty of entering the kingdom of God if
one has riches, though only in the Gospel of Luke, in the parable
of Dives and Lazarus, is a rich man described as being punished
for his wealth. He feasted sumptuously while at his gate a beggar
waited for crumbs. Thus the rich man received good things,
Lazarus bad things. After death their positions will be reversed. A
similar tale was told among ancient Egyptians,[10] but presumably
Jesus was capable of modifying various kinds of materials. The
parable reflects Luke's hostility toward wealth, perhaps also Jesus'
critical attitude.

Communism at Jerusalem?

According to Luke's book of Acts the earliest Christians at Jerusalem (but only there) practiced a form of communism: "No one
said that any of the things he possessed was his own, but they had
everything in common" (Acts 4:32–35, 2:44–45).[11] When famine
cut into their funds the church of Antioch gave the support
needed (11:27–30). There were some difficulties in the "daily distribution" (6:1–6). Kirsopp Lake thought that Luke misunderstood what evidence he had and was really describing "organized
charity" at Jerusalem.[12] He also suggested that at Jerusalem they
"broke their bread with gladness" (Acts 2:46) just because they
were using up their accumulated capital. More recently Hans
Conzelmann has called the picture "an ideal [or idealized] one."[13]
According to Conzelmann, Luke set forth what little he knew
about Jerusalem in the light of communistic groups either real—
the Essenes, the Qumran people—or ideal—as in philosophers'
pictures of future utopias or of primitive mankind. The closest
parallels occur in portrayals of the early Pythagoreans, whom the

Jewish historian Josephus compared to the Essenes.[14] The second-century satirist Lucian describes Christians as "considering everything common property." He adds that "any charlatan or trickster who comes among them quickly acquires sudden wealth by imposing on simpletons";[15] but his account may be based on nothing more than the book of Acts. Later Christians thought Luke's account was historical and usually regarded the apostolic age as a time of heroic virtue. The late first-century *Didache* may be an exception. The author of that work urges readers to share everything with brothers in need and not say "It is private property" (4.8); at the same time, they are to watch their step: "Let your alms sweat in your hands until you find out to whom you are giving" (1.6). Neither Luke nor the author of the *Didache* says anything about the ways in which the funds used for distribution were to be accumulated.

We find little concern for capital formation in the environment of the peasants, fishermen, and tax collectors of Palestine. To find a world more like our own we must turn to the "capitalists" of the Roman world, who were as rich as any of the Herodian kings in Palestine, and consider the ways in which they acquired capital and often subsequently lost it. This after all is a major aspect of the world in which Christianity arose.

Accumulation and Preservation of Wealth at Rome

The Roman Empire emerged out of the republic very shortly before the rise of Christianity, and in both republic and empire the accumulation of wealth was a fact of life. Some Romans were richer than all but kings and oriental potentates before the nineteenth century. In lists of the richest Romans,[16] half the individuals are senators, men who usually inherited wealth; but the others are more significant for our purposes because they somehow created or at least multiplied their capital.

Everyone mentions Crassus as the richest Roman of the republic. He had inherited a few millions but at his peak, even after making many gifts, he possessed 170 million sesterces[17] and went

17

so far as to claim that "no one was rich who could not support an army out of his fortune."[18] Crassus had gained much of his wealth by timely purchases of confiscated properties at low prices, or of buildings on fire or in danger of fire. He was a real estate speculator. He obviously retained much of what he gained and used it for further speculation—and for supporting his army, which did not save him from being killed in 53 B.C.

Private fortunes originated in diverse ways. Quite a few owed their existence to imperial favor; for example, Augustus gave an old comrade-in-arms ten million sesterces, which he sensibly invested in Italian land. Though this man's only son tried to murder him,[19] he still left a fortune of a hundred million.[20] Augustus' successor Tiberius despised those who could not keep the money Augustus had bestowed. A senator asked him for funds because of his relative poverty. Though Augustus had given him a million, "in these different times," the senator said, he "had been able to inherit nothing and acquire nothing," and his sons would have to leave the Senate. Tiberius reluctantly gave the four sons 200,000 sesterces apiece but spoke to the father about self-reliance. "If a man is to have nothing to hope or fear from himself, industry will languish and indolence thrive, and we shall have the whole population waiting carefree for relief, incompetent to help itself and a burden on us." In spite of the speech and the gifts, the family "kept sinking lower into shameful poverty," says Tacitus.[21] Their problem was viewed as loss of status rather than lack of capital. The emperor's praise of self-reliance and frugality contrasts oddly with what the prosenatorial historians have to say about the accumulation and loss of wealth around this time. Another unfortunate millionaire was said to have had an estate so large that it drew the attention of the emperor. Tiberius demanded to be his sole heir and then drove him to suicide.[22] Another version of the story, however, relates that Augustus gave him 400 million but his ex-slave managers stole it all.[23]

Not everyone, obviously, was faring well in the early empire. In the case of the Lollii we hear of a founder who accumulated capital through corrupt provincial government, then had to commit suicide. His son could still become consul, but the son's daughter wasted inordinate amounts on luxuries and was finally murdered. Marcus Lollius, consul in 21 B.C., was the one who founded the fortune by looting three eastern provinces but then "disgraced himself by taking gifts from oriental kings and finally drank poison." Though his son became consul, the family's decline resumed under Caligula. The granddaughter Lollia Paulina wore emeralds and pearls worth forty million, left by her grandfather and perhaps the gift of the kings. She was the wife of a senator A.D. 38 when Caligula forced her to enter into marriage with him. He soon tired of her, but a decade later she tried to marry Claudius after his wife Messalina had been executed, seeking help from astrologers, magicians, and an oracle. Claudius' niece won the contest and prosecuted Lollia for trying to get supernatural aid. Lollia's whole fortune was then confiscated, except for five million, and the officer who escorted her into banishment made sure that she committed suicide.[24] This story, worthy of daytime television, illuminates some of the sources and vicissitudes of first-century wealth.

The courtiers of both Claudius and Nero amassed huge fortunes. In 54 Claudius died and so did the very rich freedman Narcissus, whose estate of 400 million sesterces was confiscated after his death.[25] Only a little poorer was the ex-slave Pallas,[26] who plainly served both Claudius and himself. While he was financial secretary to the emperor, a grateful Senate voted him honors and fifteen million. He refused the money but accepted a bronze plaque that praised his "antique frugality."[27] Under Nero he lost his influence and resigned his office, reasonably stipulating that "there should be no back investigation of any of his actions, and his accounts with the state were to be taken as balanced."[28] Nero had him executed seven years later, however, and his fortune—confiscated—amounted to 300 million.[29] Another of these courtiers had 200 or 300 million and was considered a typical multimillionaire.[30] Conceivably the figure of 300 million is conventional; in the early second century, according to Plutarch, an amount near this was thought to constitute the largest private fortune.[31] These courtiers, with the possible exception of Pallas, owed their fortunes not to capital formation but to imperial favor.

A few smaller fortunes provide a little information about sources and investment. An ex-slave of a private individual may have had fewer opportunities for gain, but a certain Caecilius Isidorus came to be worth more than 60 million. He left that much in cash, in addition to 4,116 slaves, 3,600 yoke of oxen, and 257,000 cattle.[32] Such an estate reflects not only capital formation in the economic sense but also the wealth conferred by the ownership of capital. Physicians, often freedmen, did well in this period. Under Claudius several of them retained their fees and gifts and are said to have left estates of 30 million.[33] (The figure of 30 million may also be a stock figure, for fortunes of 30 million are mentioned on five separate occasions in the *Satyricon* of Petronius.[34]) Pliny also names a Greek astrologer-physician from Marseilles who had nearly 20 million.[35] An ex-slave who became a grammarian under Claudius had an income of 400,000 sesterces from his school and almost as much from his property. Here, it seems, we find a genuine capital-former, for he established shops for ready-made clothing and also owned vineyards in which he sometimes worked himself. One vine he grafted yielded 300 bunches of grapes.[36]

The motivation and methods of the whole class of millionaires is depicted in Petronius' *Satyricon,* which contains an imaginary but realistic portrait of an ex-slave now rich. Trimalchio proposes to erect a tombstone insisting upon his energy, his strength, and his trustworthiness. He came up from nothing, left 30 million, and never listened to a philosopher. To be sure, he married 10 million, but his virtue had made him rich. "Sound sense makes the man, everything else is rubbish. I buy low and sell high. People may tell you something different, but my frugality has brought me to this prosperity." And in general: "Believe me: if you have a penny you are worth a penny; what you have is what you will be valued at. So it is that your friend who was a frog is now a king."[37]

The ideas of the senator and philosopher Seneca about capital formation were close to those of Trimalchio. In his moral epistles Seneca frequently refers to the creation of wealth. Sometimes he is a conventional moralist, as when he notes that "money falls into the hands of some men like a denarius dropping into a sewer" or with Stoic philosophers condemns the rise of avarice.[38] Perhaps more originally, he can ask why money "always inspires a man with a greater love for itself " and answer that "he who has more begins to be able to have [still] more."[39] He tells about the career of Gaius Senecio, devoted to making more. "It is easier to improve one's status than to start out," he says, "for money comes slowly where there is poverty . . . but Senecio knew both how to make money and how to keep it—either skill could have made him rich." The tragedy of Senecio lay not in his wealth but in the fact that in spite of his extensive investments he died suddenly.[40] This Senecio was an old-fashioned, hard-working Roman, and so was the senator Volusius Saturninus, who left more than 300 million. He was even richer than Seneca, and his fortune was acquired by "long frugality" whereas Seneca's came from Nero's gift of "gardens, money for loans, and villas." He lived ninety-three years, had a remarkable fortune gained by "honorable means" (obviously the same as "long frugality"), and enjoyed the friendship of many emperors. This Volusius owed his start to his father, who died A.D. 20 and was the first "accumulator of resources" in the family.[41]

How was one to invest for income and profit? Seneca tells how a millionaire would worry about his diversified investments: at one point he anxiously awaited mail from Alexandria because for some time he had experienced neither losses nor gains from his Egyptian holdings and wanted news about them.[42] These were not trivial holdings; a century later Egyptian papyri refer to them by his name,[43] and in the year 61 he had such large sums on loan in Britain that a revolt seems to have been triggered when he tried to call in his forty million sesterces.[44] In any event, like his contemporaries Seneca took lending at interest for granted and mentions a rich man, apparently typical, who had income from crops on his large farm and from interest on loans as well.[45] The historian Tacitus goes so far as to claim that "the curse of usury [that is, lending at interest] is inveterate in Rome, a constant source of sedition and discord."[46] Certainly the satirists agree that such lending was widespread. Martial tells of a man with many acres and houses, as well as numerous debtors paying in to his cash account,[47] and Petronius describes a millionaire's account book with an entry concerning ten million sesterces that could not be lent and were being returned to the cash box.[48] Early in the next century Trajan's friend the senator Pliny the Younger had about 20 million[49] mostly in land, though he too lent money. He could easily borrow 3 million, he says, and his mother-in-law's cash was available to him. He kept track of his properties, watched rates of interest, and tried to diversify geographically in order to avoid risk.[50] Martial tells of someone who has lent 3.2 million to six individuals and enjoys a net income of 3 million from apartments and farms as well as another 600,000 from flocks at Parma.[51] This situation, which is similar to Pliny's, does not look imaginary. Both millionaires clearly tried to preserve and increase their capital. Not everyone was so careful, of course. The early first-century senator Gavius Apicius was a famous gourmand who spent 100 million on parties and had only 10 million left.[52] Not surprisingly, he was considered a prime example of a spendthrift.

In the long run Seneca did not keep his fortune either, for Nero forced him to commit suicide after leaving his 300 million to him.[53] Rich and conspicuous Romans like these were, of course, exceptional. There must have been many more who quietly accumulated capital and, like the provincial millionaires known only from inscriptions on the public buildings they donated, did not attract attention by scandal or confiscation. There are enough examples of capital formation (in the sense of trying to amass wealth) to suggest that many more Greeks and Romans were engaged in it.

An early Christian, however, would not have found the lives, fortunes, misfortunes, and fates of these rich Romans attractive. Though not all Christians shared the ideas of the book of Revelation, some could readily applaud its picture of the destruction of Babylon (Rome), the city that had given wealth to "the merchants of the earth" and "all who had ships at sea" (Rev. 18:11, 17), notoriously because of luxury trades (18:12–13). All this would be devastated and burned before the new Jerusalem came down from heaven. Many Christians treated Revelation as allegory, but others took it as literal prophecy of an impending event: God's judgment on a rich and luxury-loving civilization.

The Apostle Paul and His Gospel of Work

When Christians—notably the apostle Paul—went out into the Graeco-Roman world they did not immediately encounter Roman magnates, nor could they expect their converts to be enthusiastic supporters of the Jerusalem "saints" we have discussed. Indeed, Paul made a strenuous effort to collect funds for them, with varying levels of success. He also had to insist, to the Thessalonians and the Corinthians, that he always supported himself by working with his own hands. He may be contrasting such manual labor with his own usual pursuits, or those of his converts, or those of the Jerusalem Christians; we cannot be sure. In any case, he urges the converts to work in this way, and 2 Thessalonians 3:6–13 (whether his or not) presents his own work as a model for them. According to Acts 18:3 he was a tentmaker.

To be sure, like Jesus himself Paul insists that because "the form of this world is passing away," "those who buy should live as if they had no goods and those who deal with the world as if they had no dealings with it" (1 Cor. 7:30–31). The appointed time before the end "has grown very short" (7:29).

Yet he insists that apostles ("humanly speaking") are like soldiers who never serve at their own expense, or farmers who raise grapes for a share in the crop, or herdsmen who share in the milk. These analogies are confirmed by the law of Moses, viewed as binding (9:7–9), and point toward this question: "If we have sown spiritual good among you, is it too much if we reap your material benefits?" (9:11). When he claims that he is not seeking the Corinthians' money but their very selves, he says that "children should not lay up for their parents but parents for their children." His use of the word *thesaurizo,* to lay up a store, is significant in relation to children and parents. He believes in such savings—though he does not have capital formation in mind, since he goes on to speak of the expenditure of himself on behalf of these "children" (2 Cor. 12:14–15). Elsewhere he goes into detail ("a human example") about wills, codicils, and trustees under wills when he discusses the status of the Mosaic law (Gal. 3:15–18, 4:1–3). Such analogies point to the continuation of human society.

"Humanly," Paul has financial problems with his congregations. In 1 Corinthians 4 he calls himself a steward of the mysteries of God and adds that stewards must be trustworthy (as we have seen). He then adds, "I could not care less about being judged by you or any human court. I do not judge myself; though I have nothing on my conscience, I am not justified by this [for] he who judges me is the Lord" (4:1–4). It looks as though he had been suspected of inadequate accounting. He refuses to have his accounts audited; God will audit them. Greek cities required audits, but Paul was not willing to be bound by human auditors at Corinth. Clearly he knows about accounting and profit-and-loss, and he urges Christians not to engage in lawsuits. It is better to suffer a loss or even be defrauded than to sue (1 Cor. 6:7–8). Paul's main purpose is to prevent lawsuits before pagan judges; but he urges not suing at all. Elsewhere, when he insists that his achievements in Judaism had lost their meaning for him, he says that "whatever gain I had I counted as loss" (Phil. 3:7). Frank Beare noted that "we might almost adopt here the very words of Aristotle: 'These terms "loss" and "gain" are borrowed from the language of voluntary barter.'"[54]

Other New Testament Sources

The later pastoral letters to Timothy and Titus criticize "love of money" and "greed for gain." They urge readers to be content with their food and clothing and insist with Greek moralists that "love of money is the root of all evil" (1 Tim. 6:6–10). At the same time, elders who are also administrators are to receive double pay (5:17). The denunciation of "braided hair or gold or pearls or costly attire" (2:9) suggests a social setting lower than that of the rich Romans we mentioned earlier. Lollia Paulina was no Christian, but she may have had petty Christian imitators.

In the epistle of James, canonical only in the third century and severely criticized by Luther, we hear of a man "with gold rings and in fine clothing" who is treated too well by a church (James 2:1–5). The rich are oppressors (2:6) and ultimately they will be severely punished for their wealth and for having defrauded their laborers (5:1–5). James also dislikes traders' plans to go abroad and spend a year in making money. They should not plan so far in advance, for life is uncertain (4:13–15). In any event, "friendship with the world is enmity with God" (4:4).

Christian Ideas in the Second Century

The so-called Apostolic Fathers, who in general wrote just after the New Testament, express practical ideas. The *Epistle of Barnabas* has to warn its readers not to "associate with or imitate people who do not know how to get their food by toil and sweat but plunder the property of others. Going about in apparent simplicity of heart, they watch to see whom they may rob" (10.4). Hermas, the author of the *Shepherd,* is a small businessman who supposes that more successful competitors "deny the Lord because of wealth and their business." He claims that they "merely believed and were wrapped up in business and wealth and heathen friendships and many other occupations of this world." Indeed, the larger the business the greater the sin. "Those who work at many things also commit many sins, occupied with their business and in no way serving their Lord."[55]

Toward the end of the second century two prominent Christians, Irenaeus of Lyons and Clement of Alexandria, discussed the origin of the wealth that Christians held. Irenaeus was not enthusiastic about such wealth. If they had had it before their conversion, they had acquired it either by avarice or by gift from pagan parents, relatives, or friends. In such cases it was based on injustice. If it came after conversion, they were acquiring it in business, trying to gain the upper hand over their partners in either selling or buying. In other words, the acquisition of all property was based on injustice (basically a Platonic view), though Irenaeus does not ask Christians to give it up. Like the Israelites leaving Egypt, they must "spoil the Egyptians" (Exod. 12:35–36), that is, make use of what property they have acquired in the pagan world.[56]

Clement viewed the acquisition of property only a little more favorably. He thought that before conversion wealth can have come from work and thrift (which Irenaeus called avarice). Or perhaps God, the "distributor of fortune" (a classical expression) may have set someone in a rich family. In spite of these concessions, Clement claims that "all possessions are by nature unjust, when a man holds them as absolutely his own and does not set them in the common fund for those in need." His pendulum swings again when he argues that "out of this injustice it is possible to perform a just and saving act." Indeed, to give great wealth away is harmful because it restricts opportunities to do good.[57] By the fifth century we find Theodoret, a bishop in the East, insisting that "one must admire God for having organized things so wisely in giving wealth to one, industry to another." Since class distinctions are divinely ordered, the accumulation of wealth can have neither merit nor value.[58]

Christian Attitudes toward Banking and Gambling

In the patristic period, disapproval of wealth was combined with practical toleration. In the third century we find bishops of Rome, Antioch, and Alexandria vigorously engaged in banking, whether for the churches' benefit or their own.[59] (Earlier evidence from Pontus and Africa shows Christians handling the deposits of others.[60]) Theory was obviously not identical with practice, and this point must be considered when bishops and others denounce the wealth of individuals but usually not that of the church.

Christians generally disapproved of games of chance involving money. A second-century critic of the sectarian Montanist prophets asked if a real prophet ever played at tables with dice or, for that matter, lent money at interest.[61] Various authors and synods later condemned the practice, and usury as well—which we have already seen criticized by Roman moralists.

The Late Roman Empire and After

From the early years of the empire the emperors tended to debase the coinage, but Constantine stabilized it with his new solidus,

EARLY CHRISTIANITY AND CAPITAL

a coin that outlasted the Roman empire. Relative peace under Constantine and his successors meant that capital could be accumulated, and the wealth of the rich was taxed lightly. Bishops and other preachers of the new imperial church, however, strenuously criticized the rich both new and old. The most prominent such preacher was John Chrysostom, who advocated a social program with communist tinges; he was banished for criticizing the empress.[62] Communistic ideas enjoyed a modest vogue at the fringes of Christian life and teaching. In the second century an adolescent enthusiast named Epiphanes wrote *On Justice* to denounce private property and monogamy, arguing that God provided food to be shared by all animals and arranged for all to reproduce instinctively.[63] His naive discussion seems to assume that food and, for that matter, clothing is produced spontaneously, and reflects a literal interpretation of some passages in the Sermon on the Mount (Matt. 6:25–32). The basic "late antique" Christian viewpoint, however, was not communistic but either monastic (sharing within a limited group) or neutral toward wealth. The church laid emphasis on distribution rather than production, on charity rather than thrift. The authoritative sayings of Jesus, like the letters of Paul, encouraged this emphasis. There was little occasion to discuss the accumulation of capital except by denouncing acquisitiveness.

The nature of the ancient world's economy is equally important. M. I. Finley points out that at Rome "the strong drive to acquire wealth was not translated into a drive to create capital; stated differently, the prevailing mentality was acquisitive but not productive."[64] The moral criticisms of the church were directed against the acquisitive mind-set, not against economic systems or programs. Love of God and neighbor were violated by greed and avarice, no matter what the economy. The use of such language, however, did little to illuminate individual or even social situations. To a surprising degree the medieval economy was continuous with that of the Roman Empire, though Christians gradually gave up their condemnation of usury (that is, taking interest on loans) since it conflicted with the need to borrow money for the embryonic capitalist enterprises of the thirteenth and fourteenth centuries. Theologians gradually recognized the necessity for redefining usury, and did so with almost total success once distinctions were drawn between loans for production and loans for consumption.[65] Capitalists, with or without a capitalist system, could now lend or venture money as they had done in the old Roman world.

The church both ancient and medieval respected private property. The 38th Article of Religion of the Church of England (printed in the *Book of Common Prayer*) simply follows the central tradition when it insists that "the Riches and Goods of Christians are not common, as touching the right, title and possession of the same; as certain Anabaptists do falsely boast." In an equally traditional manner, the article balances this statement with the exhortation that "notwithstanding, every man ought, of such things as he possesseth, liberally to give alms to the poor, according to his ability."

The Influence of Calvin

Modern discussions of capital formation are expected to deal with the ideas of John Calvin, supposedly the founder of modern Protestant ethical doctrine approving capital formation (that is, the accumulation of wealth).[66] Both Max Weber and Ernst Troeltsch discussed the topic at length, and we do not wish to repeat their discussions. Troeltsch's comments on work, vocation, and the accumulation of capital seem to show, however, that Calvin is less distinctive than one might suppose. "The Calvinist concept of 'calling' . . . raised the ordinary work of one's profession (within one's vocation) and the ardour with which secular work was prosecuted to the level of a religious duty in itself; from a mere method of providing for material needs it became an end in itself, providing scope for the exercise of faith within the labour of the 'calling.' That gave rise to that ideal of work for work's sake which forms the intellectual and moral assumption which lies behind the modern bourgeois way of life"[67]—and, we add, is certainly found in the background of the apostle Paul. "Labour and profit," Troeltsch continues in his summary of Calvin's ideas, "were never intended for purely personal interest. The capitalist is always a steward of the gifts of God whose duty is to *increase his capital* [italics mine] and utilize it for the sake of Society as a whole, retaining for himself only that amount which is necesssary to provide for his own needs."[68] We may add that except for the term "capital," the ideas come from the Old Testament and the Pauline epistles. It was not Calvin who first said, "Whatever your task, work heartily, as serving the Lord and not men" (Col. 3:23).

In any event, an ethic for capital creation can hardly be based just on selected biblical texts or theological statements or committee resolutions. The whole history of Christian teaching shows that it is not so based. Christian teaching since the patristic period has relied on principles that try to balance or maintain in tension the basic proclamations of the gospel, the insights of the Christian tradition, and the problems and answers of people today; in other words, on scripture, tradition, and reason. Though the terms always need definition and correlation and some modification in the light of circumstances, through the centuries they have served to maintain and reinterpret the church's teaching from one period to another. All three principles involve some historical understanding; that is, gaining insight into the circumstances in which each has made its contribution. The problem is to find the right proportions, and to realize how our understanding of each aspect is to be combined with our understanding of the others. Though self-interest is present in institutions as in persons and in their interpretations, some measure of balanced exegesis may finally emerge. No single principle is likely to be right.

Economics and Justice:
A Jewish Example

When one speaks of economics and justice, three distinct areas should be delineated at the outset: the just economics of production, the just economics of distribution, and the just economics of rectification.[1] This delineation, however, should not be taken as final in any sense; it merely identifies three closely connected spheres of one activity that is essential for human society. None of these spheres can be adequately understood without close consideration of its relation to the others.

Society's distribution of the things necessary for the bodily needs of its members cannot justly be conducted on the basis of a strictly arithmetic equality. If a society has, let us say for purposes of simple illustration, a hundred members, the things possessed by that society cannot be justly divided into a hundred equal parts. Such a rigidly egalitarian distribution corresponds neither to need nor to desert. Applied to food, for example, this type of distribution would undersatisfy a farm worker, giving him too little for his bodily needs, and it would oversatisfy a child, giving her too much. Such egalitarian distribution would quickly liquidate that society's things—a process only appropriate when there is no concern for the needs of the present, much less any projection toward the future.

Arithmetic equality is only appropriate in the sphere of rectification, that is, the restoration of private property misappropriated in one way or another. In this case, a person's claim on a portion of society's things is based on past distribution alone; the question of present need or desert is irrelevant. Rectification, unlike distribution, is only concerned with things as possessions—what one already has or should have. Those societies that do not permit their members the private possession of at least some things cannot practice true rectifying justice.[2]

Distribution must be proportional rather than equal if it is to be just and accomplish its intended purpose. To return to our example of the distribution of food, a farm worker might require two or more times as much food as a child. A just distribution would allocate food to the farm worker and the child in proportion to their respective needs. The equality lies in treating the different needs with equal consideration, not in trying to equalize them.[3]

Nevertheless, if the respective needs of the members of a society were the only criterion of distribution, such a distribution would eventually liquidate that society's things. The present satisfaction of needs in no way provides for the future replenishment of the things distributed. Distribution according to need alone could only be sustained if the source of necessary things were infinite and always at hand. If this were true, then there would be no requirement to distinguish between the needs of someone who produces more of society's things and someone who produces less. As individuals, both might expend the same amount of energy and have the same needs. However, since a society must be concerned with continuing into the future, and since the source of necessary things is finite and usually not at hand, distribution is also based on desert. Those who produce more of what is needed by the society are given more than those who produce less. These rewards, even more than being recompense for past productivity, are incentives for future productivity. It would seem that anyone who does not at least partially correlate the economics of distribution and the economics of production is operating under an illusion of infinite supply and immediate availability. Such an illusion is often the indulgence of those who have never had to work for a living.

Just distribution, in any society, requires a balance between need on the one hand and desert on the other. Distribution based on need alone would lead to the eventual liquidation of the things necessary for human life. It is too unselective, providing no incentives for production. Conversely, distribution based on desert alone is too exclusive. It fails to provide for those who are not productive, those who cannot supply anything that the members of society need. The needs of these people, if one strictly follows the logic of distribution by desert alone, can only be met by the largesse of the more productive members of society. Since such largesse would not be required by any objective social norms, it would not be subject to any criteria of justice.

A concept of justice based solely on desert would, indeed, destroy what many consider the most basic social reality, the family. The production of material necessities is important, but it is surely not the primary activity of the family. The family is much more than an economic unit. Its primary activity is intimate interpersonal contact. Family life includes those members who are not productive by any measurable standard: the very young, the very old, the infirm, the handicapped—even the unborn. Their needs far outstrip their economic deserts. Since none of us are totally assured of our own future productivity, we desire family life. The family is where we are accepted for what we are rather than for what we make. Society must keep a balance between the needs of the hearth and the deserts of the marketplace, between being and making.[4]

Biblical Economics

A theologian rooted in the Hebrew Bible will have difficulty formulating a theory of human productivity and justice because the Hebrew Bible seems to be concerned only with the just distribution and redistribution (rectification) of necessary things. God is presented as the true and faithful producer and provider of the things we need, and God's provision of these things is presented as a matter of grace, not justice. Thus, the people of Israel were fed manna for forty years in the wilderness by the grace of God alone. This experience is taken to be the paradigm of the Covenant through which the Lord is related to his people.

> And he afflicted you and made you hungry and fed you the manna, which you had not known and your fathers had not known, so as to let you know that humans (*ha'adam*) do not live by bread alone, but rather on everything that proceeds out of the mouth of the Lord do humans live. (Deut. 8:3)

Humans are warned about taking pride in their productive accomplishments, since all wealth comes from God for his own covenantal purposes.

> And if you say: "My strength and the power of my hand have produced all this wealth (*hayil*) for me," then you shall remember the Lord your God, that it is he who gives you strength to produce wealth in order to uphold his Covenant. (Deut. 8:17–18)

This does not mean that God simply supplies all the needs of humans without any effort on their part. Even in the garden of Eden, the first humans were required to work (*l'obdah*) the garden from which they were to eat (Gen. 2:15).[5] Bread, mentioned in the verse from Deuteronomy quoted above, is the prime example of that which humans can only eat "by the sweat of your brow" (Gen. 3:19). The fact that humans do not live by bread alone does not mean that they can live without it. The Lord is seen as being like a loving father whose assignment of activities to his children is not meant to make himself indispensable, but rather to enable them to participate in his care of the family, living together upon the ancestral estate. Making bread is one such necessary activity. When humans think their productive powers are fully sufficient for their needs, bodily and spiritual, they are attempting to live "by bread alone."[6]

The Covenant between God and his people involves a set of responsibilities on the part of the people. God chose his people to participate in a Covenant upon the land he has given them to be their home. The Covenant places a set of responsibilities on the people, as can be seen in the following biblical passage:

> When you come to the land which I give you, the land shall rest as a Sabbath for the Lord. Six years you shall plant your field . . . and you shall gather in its produce. And in the seventh year it shall be a complete Sabbath for the land, . . . your field you shall not plant. . . . The Sabbath of the land shall be for you [plural]: for your [singular] food and for that of . . . your hirelings and tenants. (Lev. 25:2–4, 6)

The prime responsibility, of course, is to God: the land is his and the people are only there as "sojourners and tenants along with me" (*'immadi,* Lev. 25:23). Hence, they can never regard the land or its produce as their possession in any final sense.

This prime responsibility includes the following sub-responsibilities: responsibility for the land, responsibility toward other people, and responsibility toward one's own future.

The responsibility for the land is to allow it to refresh itself every seventh year, to allow it a measure of freedom from human control. In the same way, a servant is never truly a slave because he or she must be allowed the freedom of Sabbath rest just as much as his or her master (Exod. 20:10).[7] As in Eden, the land is to be both "worked and kept" (*le-shomrah,* Gen. 2:15). The human guardians are prior in God's concern to the land itself; but that priority does not entail unlimited human lordship over the land.

The responsibility toward other people means that the produce of the land is to be shared. During the seventh year all are to share the land's produce; but even before the seventh year, neighbors are seen as participants in a family-type organism where the strong help the weak for the sake of the well-being of the whole. "And when your brother becomes impoverished and his means decrease when he is with you, you shall strengthen him as a sojourner and a tenant; and your brother shall live with you" (*'imakh,* Lev. 25:35). The reason given for this mutual responsibility is covenantal. "For the children of Israel are servants of mine; my servants they are whom I took out of the land of Egypt; I am the Lord your God" (Lev. 25:55).[8]

Only at the level of responsibility toward one's own future is there any indication of an imperative to be productive. Even here, though, the imperative is not direct but only by implication. Thus, the promise of God's providing during the fallow seventh year is presented as a divine assurance in the face of understandable human anxiety: "What will we eat during the seventh year? Indeed, we will not be planting or harvesting our produce" (*tebu'atenu,* Lev. 25:20). The implication is that during the other six years of this cycle we should be planting and harvesting, and that the results of this labor will be ours. In the same way, the Israelite is not only commanded to cease from his or her labor on the seventh day, but is also commanded to "do all your labor" on the other six days (Exod. 20:9.[9]) One's efforts to assure one's future wealth are not directed toward an unlimited future, whether individual, as in the case of modern capitalism, or collective, as in the case of modern socialism. The future is limited by the seven-year cycle. In the case of land possessed in addition to one's own ancestral portion, that cycle is extended sevenfold, to the fifty-year cycle of the jubilee (Lev. 25:8–13).

The maldistribution of wealth—some getting too much and others too little—is considered to be an intolerable imbalance, requiring rectification. That rectification calls for both divine grace and human justice. Those who lack the material necessities of life are encouraged to cry unto the Lord, who assures them that "I shall hear because I am gracious" (Exod. 22:26). After all, God is the ultimate source of all those things humans (and the rest of creation) need (Ps. 104:13–15). Nevertheless, the more fortunate members of the community are not to stand idly by while their less fortunate brethren simply wait for God's mercy. They themselves are required to provide those material needs, and they are subject to severe divine punishment if they do not act justly toward those in need (Exod. 22:22–23).

The preferred way of providing aid seems to be the lending of necessities, or money for necessities, to the less fortunate members of the community (Exod. 22:24–26; Lev. 25:35–37; Deut. 15:7–10). A loan, by definition, is given in order to be subsequently repaid. Maimonides, in his comprehensive treatment of the entire biblical and rabbinic system of aid for the less fortunate members of the community, eloquently emphasizes that the purpose of all such aid is to create conditions whereby the recipient will "not have to ask other human beings for aid."[10]

The wider implications of the primacy of the loan can best be seen when contrasted with two other means for the redistribution of wealth: charity and state welfare.

The most obvious alternative to the loan is simple charity: giving necessities, or money for necessities, with no strings attached— a gift pure and simple. Such magnanimity would seem to an act of true *imitatio Dei*—imitation of God, whose grace cannot, of course, ever be repaid by its recipients. This interpretation, however, is inconsistent with the logic of the Covenant. God is our superior, whereas we are all supposed to be essentially equal before him. The maldistribution of wealth, whatever the cause might be, is a threat to the Covenant if it entails too great a disparity between the rich and the poor members of the community. That disparity is not relieved by human charity, inasmuch as the recipients of charity become the dependents of those giving it. Even though their bodily needs might be temporarily satisfied, the charity they have received will tend to make them passive. The objects of charity are more likely to lose their covenantal dignity than those who are merely subjected to poverty. There are times when charity is mandated; however, it is not meant to be the primary means for redistribution of wealth in the context of the Covenant.[11]

The second alternative to the loan is one with which we moderns are quite familiar: state welfare, which bypasses interpersonal transactions and simply redistributes wealth from a centralized base. Why depend on unpredictable goodwill when redistribution of wealth can be programmed by the state? Here an example from the career of Joseph is illuminating. After the seven years of plenty predicted by Pharaoh's dreams, which Joseph so astutely interpreted, the Egyptian people did not have enough food stored up to sustain themselves during the seven years of famine that followed.

In desperation they begged Joseph as Pharaoh's prime minister: "Buy us and our land with food, and we and our land will be Pharaoh's slaves" (Gen. 47:19). In this act of mass surrender one can see a process of equalization (what a modern tyranny called *Gleichschaltung*). And, after all, was not Pharaoh only the personification of the state; hence, would not being his slaves subsequently redound to the benefit of them all? In theory this sounds all right, but in practice personifications do not act, only real persons do. State ownership of all wealth can only lead to the tyranny of the few who actually run the state over the many who serve the state. Such a state quickly develops its own bureaucracy with a life and interests of its own. Such a political and economic system is inconsistent with the covenantal sovereignty of God alone and the personal interdependence of his people.

The fear that such a tyranny might occur in Israel, as in neighboring societies—societies not participating in the Covenant with the Lord—lies at the heart of the antimonarchial argument presented repeatedly in the Bible. Thus, when warning the people of Israel of the likely results of their desire for a strong centralized monarchy, the prophet Samuel emphasized that

> this will be the way of the king (*mishpat ha-melekh*) who will rule over you: he will take your sons and use them for his own cavalry . . . he will take your best fields and vineyards and olive groves and give them to his servants . . . and you will be his servants. (1 Sam. 8:11, 14, 17)[12]

The prophet says that wealth will be redistributed, but not at all equally. Rather, those who prove to be more useful to the power of the state will be more greatly rewarded, irrespective of the true needs of all the people.[13] Some servants will get a lot more than others.

The just redistribution of wealth, in accordance with the principles of the Covenant, is thus best accomplished by loans. Charity exacerbates the class divisions between the rich and the poor; centralized state redistribution of wealth creates a new type of inequality, difficult to dislodge because it is backed up by political tyranny and its accompanying military might.[14]

The Sabbatical Year and the Cancellation of Loans

The sabbatical year was prescribed to be a time when the people of Israel were to refrain from making claims on the land of Israel. The land was to lie fallow. It was also a time when the people were to refrain from making claims on one another. All loans during that year were to be canceled. However, the anticipation that loans would be canceled during the seventh year was not allowed to be a factor in deciding whether to make a loan.

> When there is among you one of your brothers who is needy (*'ebyon*) . . . do not make your heart stubborn and remove your aid. . . . Beware, lest there be something base (*beli'al*) in your heart saying, "The seventh year, the year of release is nearing." And you will become stingy with your needy brother and you will not give to him. Then he will call unto the Lord about you and you will be guilty. . . . For those in need will not totally cease from the midst of the land. (Deut. 15:7–9, 11)[15]

We see from this quotation that the more fortunate members of the covenanted community must always be aware that lending to their less fortunate brethren could, in effect, turn out to be giving them charity.

It is plausible to assume that the normal situation at that time was as follows. Those borrowing from others were likely to be people whose harvests from their own land had been too meager to provide them and their families with the bare necessities of life. Borrowing from a more fortunate neighbor probably meant taking a loan until the next harvest. The produce should then be sufficient to provide the material things needed by the borrower and enough of a surplus to repay the debt, or at least part of the debt, the remainder to be repaid from the surplus of the next harvest or harvests. If this could not be done, however, and the borrower had already used up any reserve upon which to draw (like the hapless people of Egypt during the time of Joseph), then by the time of the sabbatical year, when there would be no harvest for anyone, the only alternative to cancellation of the debt would be for the poor brother to indenture himself to the rich one.[16] It seems that during the sabbatical year (like the Sabbath day upon which it was explicitly modeled) covenantal mutuality took precedence over private property privileges.

Apparently this system worked on the whole until the time of Hillel the Elder, who led the Jewish people in Palestine during the latter part of the first century B.C. The Mishnah specifically mentions that this great and influential sage invented a procedure called *prosbul* to enable the repayment of loans during the sabbatical year without literal violation of the biblical law. Without this measure the system of the rich lending to the poor was in danger of coming to a halt.[17]

The Mishnah describes *prosbul* as consisting of the following formula uttered by a lender before a court and then written down and attested in a formal legal document afterward: "I herewith turn myself over to you judges X and Y in such and such a place, that any debt owed me I may collect at any time I want."[18] The court, as a political institution, was exempt from the personal commandment to cancel debts during the sabbatical year. The court also had the power to reassign property as it saw fit. The court thus had the power to demand in its own name the repayment of a loan even during the sabbatical year, and then to reassign the repaid loan to the lender. Some later rabbis were concerned with what seemed to be a radical departure from the spirit of the law by a forced interpretation of its letter. One of them, the third-century Babylonian sage and jurist Samuel of Nehardea, proclaimed that if he had the power, he would remove this institution altogether. He considered that it gave too much power to the human court. He thus termed it "the arrogance (*'ulbana*) of the judges."[19] Nevertheless, the Talmud makes it quite clear that the dispensation of *prosbul* was too deeply embedded in the Jewish legal system and the economic life of the Jewish community to be repealed.[20]

The Mishnah designates *prosbul* as one of the enactments (*taqqanot*) of Hillel intended for "the repair of the world" (*tiqqun ha'olam*), which is a rabbinic concept similar to that of *bonum commune,* where the good of society as a whole requires the adjustment of private legal rights.[21]

Why did the people during the time of Hillel refrain from lending because of the imminent approach of the sabbatical year? Why was the possibility about which the Torah had long before warned not realized until the time of Hillel?

In the most comprehensive critical monograph written to date on the *prosbul,* the Hungarian Jewish scholar Ludwig Blau argued over sixty years ago that the *prosbul* was necessary when the Jewish people in Palestine had ceased being primarily an agricultural community and had become, in response to new economic circumstances in the larger world around them, a community of craftsmen and traders. There was such a fundamental shift in the economic *Sitz im Leben* that a procedure was needed to alter the effect of the law while preserving its letter. Blau saw this as a basic conflict between religious morality and economic reality, one calling for a compromise of sorts.[22]

The fundamental shift was that loans were now no longer a response to past misfortune, closely akin to charity. Rather, loans were now a means of investment for the sake of future gain. In this new economic climate, loans were extended in order to enable a craftsman or trader to purchase equipment or stock for the sake of future profit; it would seem that loans were now more important and more prevalent than they had been heretofore. In the past, borrowers were usually those unfortunate few whose agricultural harvest had been an exception to a general situation of sufficiency, if not plenty. Thus, a situation where "you will not have to borrow" (Deut. 28:12) was considered a blessing, and one where you have to borrow, a curse (28:44). In the more commercial climate, however, loans became the rule rather than the exception. Furthermore, since commerce was not limited by the seven-year cycle of the sabbatical year system, and since commercial profit is far less predictable than annual harvests, it would seem that loans had also become more long-term than they were previously.

Earlier, the nineteenth-century Austrian Jewish scholar Isaac Hirsch Weiss had pointed out the moral dilemma that Hillel faced and ultimately resolved by his *prosbul* enactment. The dilemma was not so much the conflict between old religious law and new economic opportunities, but rather a conflict between two norms of religious law itself. On the one hand, there was the more specific norm requiring cancellation of loans during the sabbatical year. On the other hand, there was the more general norm requiring (but not forcing) the rich to lend to the poor. In the biblical context in which these two norms are juxtaposed and related to each other, it is clear that the sabbatical year is the primary concern and lending to the poor the secondary concern. The reason for this conclusion is that the sabbatical year was a reality for all, whereas the need for loans was the reality only of the poverty-stricken few. During the period of Hillel, however, there seems to have been a fundamental economic shift, so that the need for loans became more usual. Also, as we shall see, the sabbatical year itself was not the same institution during the period of the Second Temple as it had been during the period of the First Temple (before 586 B.C.). Thus, for Weiss, the moral requirement of the Covenant was to strengthen the institution of lending so that the poor would be able to survive in the new commercial economy. Hence, lending now became primary and the specifics of the sabbatical year secondary.[23] In fact, long after Hillel's enactment a Babylonian rabbi offered a philologically forced but conceptually insightful etymology of the word *prosbul.* (The word is no doubt originally Greek—indeed, Blau showed its origin in a Hellenistic legal institution—but the etymology proposed in the *Babylonian Talmud* is Aramaic, the lingua franca of the Babylonian Jews.) *Prosbul* was interpreted as being that which is beneficial to both rich and poor. The rich do not lose their money through loans not being repaid; the poor do not find that the opportunity to borrow money is "closed in their faces."[24]

The late German and then Israeli Jewish scholar Chanoch Albeck and the American Jewish scholar David Weiss Halivni have argued that although *prosbul* was an innovation, it was not without precedent in the rabbinic jurisprudence that preceded Hillel.[25] Looking at these precedents enables us to see more specifically how an ethic of production and distribution emerged out of the reinterpretation of older sources concerned primarily with an ethic of rectification and distribution.

The Sabbatical Year and the Jubilee

From the primary biblical sources dealing with the institution of the sabbatical year, we see that the system of letting the land lie fallow and canceling loans every seven years was part of a larger economic system, that of the jubilee. The jubilee system was based on the premise that every native Israelite had an ancestral portion of land within the patrimony of his own particular tribe, an inviolable allotment from the time of the conquest of Canaan under Joshua. If one needed money more than he needed his ancestral portion, he was allowed to lease his portion, the lease price being prorated according to how many years were still left before the jubilee year, which came every fiftieth year. During the jubilee year, "you shall declare liberty (*deror*) in the land to all its inhabitants; it shall be a jubilee for you. Then a man shall return to his ancestral portion (*'ahuzato*), then shall you return, each man, to his family" (Lev. 25:10).[26]

All wealth was, ultimately, inherited land. This wealth was part of a complete system whereby the entire land of Israel was under the control of all twelve original tribes of Israel. The system was an economically closed one. The people of Israel were seen as being totally dependent on God's grace and the justice they were to practice toward one another. If the entire land of Israel was not under the control of all twelve original tribes of Israel, the rabbis recognized that the jubilee system could not possibly work. The rabbis saw the operation of the system as being legally contingent on the existence of the closed system. This meant that the jubilee system ceased during the time before the destruction of the First Temple in 586 B.C., when the ten northern tribes went into Assyrian exile, never again to return to their ancestral land.[27] For these exiles, there was no assurance that one would return to his ancestral portion of the land within his own lifetime, or that his children would do so during their lifetime. Moreover, Jewish control of the land of Israel was now partial at best. Thus, there was no longer the ancient assurance that made workable an economy based on landed patrimony. The economic system under which the Jewish people were now living in postexilic Palestine and the

Diaspora was not under their control. They were now subject to larger political forces and to the larger economic forces of an international market oblivious to the laws of the Jews. Economic survival and productive growth called for reinterpretation of the revealed law. As we have seen, however, economic survival and productivity are not values in themselves. They are values only because without them the differences between the haves and the have-nots become exacerbated and the social mutuality required by the Covenant is severely curtailed.

Rabbinic interpretation also saw the biblically mandated system of the cancellation of loans in the sabbatical year as being contingent on the operation of the jubilee.[28] However, even though there was no longer a strictly biblical requirement for either institution, the rabbis, by their own biblically warranted authority, relegislated the law of the sabbatical year release as "a memorial of the sabbatical year," so that it would not be totally forgotten in practice.[29]

This is not the only example of rabbinic relegislation of a biblical institution no longer required by biblical law itself.[30] Nevertheless, even though such practices might appear the same whether based on biblical revelation or rabbinic legislation, their structure has been essentially changed. The change concerns the teleology of the legal institution.

Based on the theological principle "My thoughts are not your thoughts" (Isa. 55:8), it was always assumed that the basic fact that God's commandments are his revealed will always takes precedence over any discussion of the possible reasons for those commandments.[31] Thus, if one were to infer the purpose of a commandment, and to judge that the commandment no longer served that purpose, such a judgment would be deemed invalid. The commandment could not be repealed on the basis of such a judgment.[32] The assumption is that God's revealed will has absolute authority because it is wholly sufficient. Human reasoning, in contrast, has only relative authority because it is never wholly sufficient. When interpreting divine law, human reason is never foundational but only confirmational at best. Hearing God's voice takes precedence over reading God's mind, even when that seems possible.

With rabbinic legislation, however, the assumption is that humans can fully understand why other humans have legislated as they have.[33] It was possible, though not easy, for later rabbis to repeal the legislation of earlier rabbis.[34] Rabbinic law is based on precedent, but precedent never has the absolute authority of revelation. Even without formal repeal, later rabbinic reinterpretation of earlier rabbinic legislation could be far more radical than reinterpretation of any biblical norm.

The relegislation of the norms of the sabbatical year by the rabbis probably took place at the time of Ezra and the constitution of the Second Jewish Commonwealth. The relegislation seems to have been intended to restore the covenantal mutuality established by the original biblical revelation.[35] The difference between the original biblical revelation and the subsequently reconstituted human institution is as follows. The inference of the biblical revelation's intent could only have a hermenuetical function, one which at best could influence only certain details of practical application; whereas the intent of the human legislators, whether explicit or inferred, directly determines the full range of practical application or nonapplication.[36] In the case of the sabbatical year, a medieval gloss on the Talmud questions why the rabbis did not reconstitute the biblical institution of the jubilee as they had reconstituted the biblical institution of the sabbatical year. The answer given is that this would not be in the best economic interests of the community, inasmuch as the land would have to lie fallow for two consecutive years: the forty-ninth, sabbatical, year and the fiftieth, jubilee, year.[37] An economic concern is thus assumed to have been part of the rabbinic intent in not reconstructing the jubilee year, just as it was part of the rabbinic intent in reconstructing the sabbatical year. Concern for Jewish economic interests could be attributed to human legislators, but not to God as the giver of the biblical law. One could not transform a biblical law, or even suggest that others had transformed it, on the basis of such an inference.[38]

The recognition that God himself was no longer the immediate provider of Jewish economic well-being, as he had been when all twelve tribes of Israel lived in the land of Israel, led to a greater emphasis on human productivity. It should also be noted, however, that this development was not taken to be a cause for celebration. Lest we read modern notions of historical progress into this transition, let it be emphasized that the transition was seen as the result of divinely mandated exile, which was a punishment for sins committed when the people of Israel were in full domicile upon the land of Israel (Lev. 26:33–34). The great hope for full redemption is that God will fully restore the people of Israel to their pristine state of dependence upon his direct providence in their promised land.[39] The current situation of greater self-reliance, including greater economic self-reliance, cannot be taken as indicating the existence of what Adam Smith called "an invisible hand [promoting] an end which was no part of his [the human economic actor's] intention."[40] Rather, it indicates the absence of the invisible hand of God, which was felt to be present before the exile. This sad fact of our temporary self-reliance must be accepted as our historical reality; any attempt to ignore our current need for economic productivity can only be regarded as pseudomessianic.[41] Such pseudomessianism can be seen in the attempt to model an ethics of economic distribution primarily upon rectifying justice, that is, the attempt to represent economic justice as primarily recompense for past injustices or misfortunes.

Direct Precedents of *Prosbul*

The changed economic situation, which led Hillel to institute *prosbul*, can also be seen as the reason for two earlier norms pertaining to the cancellation of loans during the sabbatical year. The Mishnah teaches that "whoever lends money for which a deposit has been taken, and whoever turns his notes over to the court: these debts are not subject to the cancellation of the sabbatical year."[42] The Talmud explains this exception on the basis of the wording of the biblical text "what will be (*'asher yihyeh*) for you of your brother's" (Deut. 15:3), which implies that the law of release does not pertain to "something of your brother's already under your hand."[43] This can be understood if one is aware of the diminished economic importance of land and the increased economic importance of movable things.[44] When the land was the chief source of livelihood, the poor who would need loans in the event of a bad harvest would also need their possessions for their bare subsistence. The borrower's future would be seen in the immediate productivity of the land, not in the future value of things apart from the land.[45] It seems that this is why biblical law does not permit the lender to hold any collateral that the poor might offer for a loan. Any deposit of goods with the lender would only exacerbate the borrower's poverty (Exod. 22:25–26; Deut. 24:12–13).[46]

In a more commercial economy, movable things would extend beyond the immediate necessities of food, shelter, and clothing to include articles used in trade and investment. The very fact that the Mishnah sees the deposit as something that the lender keeps throughout the sabbatical year indicates that the things deposited are not necessities, since the borrower can live without them. In other words, the loan is not given because the borrower has nothing but the shirt on his back, so to speak. Rather, the loan is now more probably for the sake of investment, a risk taken by both lender and borrower in the hope that the future will yield a better income than the present. In this case, the need for the sabbatical year release from indebtedness, which in the agricultural context would make a loan into a charitable gift, would no longer be required. Redistribution determined by considerations of future productivity is fundamentally different from redistribution as a form of rectification of past misfortune. A deposit in the former case is fundamentally different from a deposit in the latter case.

As we have seen, notes turned over to the court were not subject to cancellation during the sabbatical year. The Talmud interprets the biblical words, "and what will be for you of your brother's (*'et 'ahikha*) shall you release your hand" (Deut. 15:3) as exempting someone who has already delegated the power to collect his debts to a public institution—the court—from the rule that applies to someone who deals directly with a private party— "your [singular] brother."[47] Some rabbinic sources see this ruling as being the legal basis for Hillel's enactment of *prosbul*.[48] So we might speculate upon this connection and ask how this ruling paved the way for *prosbul.*

It would seem that the ruling makes provision for individual dispensation from a general legal requirement. We might envision this in the following scenario. A lent B money before the sabbatical year. According to biblical law, B's debt to A is canceled if B could not pay it before the sabbatical year. The assumption seems to be that B's poverty, which had caused him to borrow from A in the first place, has not been alleviated by the time the sabbatical year came around. Hence, what began as a loan from A should now become a form of charity for one in extremis. However, what if the tables were turned? What if B's poverty had indeed been alleviated by the time the sabbatical year came around, but A now found himself in desperate circumstances? Rather than have A become the recipient of charity, it seems that the law made provision for him to plead hardship to the court. The judges could then collect the debt and turn it over to A, in effect exempting him from the biblical requirement to cancel all debts during the sabbatical year.

Prosbul built upon this provision by eliminating the requirement that the lender request the court to collect his debts for him. *Prosbul* enabled the lender, by a legal fiction, to act as though his debts had been taken over by the court; but in fact it was the lender who collected the debts, not the court.[49] In other words, the lender no longer had to turn his notes over to the court for collection; he had only to make a standardized statement. The court's acceptance of this statement gave him blanket authority to collect his debts himself during the sabbatical year. The earlier individualized procedure, unlike the later standardized procedure, required the lender to make a personal appearance before the court and specify the content of each of his notes. It would seem that such a personal appearance with its specific request probably entailed a personal plea of poverty. Loans in a commercial context, however, are fundamentally different from loans in an agricultural context. In the new commercial situation, loans were for the sake of investment, not for the sake of rectifying past misfortune. The element of poverty no longer seems to be the motivating factor in most cases. The requirement that one plead poverty in order to collect debts could not be met by those who had lent money to borrowers for commercial purposes. Furthermore, since loans became much more prevalent in the new commercial context, the old requirement that one appear before the court to explain one's circumstances would create a burden on the judges. *Prosbul* facilitated the whole process of lending money by eliminating what had become needless bother for both lenders and judges.

Conclusion

As has been emphasized throughout this chapter, the covenantal interdependence of the community before God constantly informed the theoretical interpretation and the practical application of the specifics of the law—in the case under discussion, the specifics of the law of the sabbatical year. Concern with economic productivity became part of the covenantal reality as long as such concern could be justified as improving the lot of the community. Such concern is, however, in opposition to that covenantal reality when it is seen as an end in itself, justifying the differences between the rich and the poor, the powerful and the powerless. The legal institution of *prosbul,* and its subsequent alternatives, allowed the new productivity introduced by commerce to be affirmed for the sake of the Covenant. By emphasizing the covenantal necessity of human mutuality before God, Jewish tradition affirmed the value of individual incentive without the glorification of individual human selfishness, and it affirmed the value of communal restraints without the glorification of collective human power. It saw both individual incentive and communal restraints as tentative human modi vivendi until the time when "the kingdom is the Lord's" (Obad. 1:21) and the present system of checks and balances will no longer be needed. However, any attempt to jump over the present requirements and to institute the kingdom of God by political means must be explicitly rejected as dangerous pseudomessianism.[50] Therefore, whatever current political and economic system most closely approximates the covenantal reality should have the support of those committed to the Jewish tradition. All the premessianic systems of human politics and economics are flawed, but some are clearly more flawed than others. The least flawed system deserves the most support as long as one is ever cognizant of the real difference between that which "will endure forever" (Isa. 40:8) and that which, like all other human systems, will surely pass away.

THREE   MICHAEL NOVAK

Wealth and Virtue:
The Development of
Christian Economic Teaching

For many centuries commerce and industry were looked upon as morally inferior occupations, and the desire to make money was frowned upon. So tight was the hold of the aristocratic classes upon the imagination of moralists, as well as upon the daily lives of persons of lower station, that morality itself was described in terms of "the noble" as distinct from the merely useful or (still lower) the pleasant. Nonetheless, beginning in the seventeenth and eighteenth centuries a group of Western European moralists—especially in Scotland—became skeptical of the moral biases of the aristocratic class. This group of moralists developed the thesis that a regime based upon commerce, pursuing plenty as well as power, offered the most reasonable route to the moral betterment of the human race. They undertook a massive transvaluation of Western values. Whereas earlier generations had considered commerce and the pursuit of wealth morally inferior, these moralists considered such pursuits morally superior to those that were the foundations of previous regimes.

This moral argument for capitalism before its triumph has been too little noted—is indeed almost entirely overlooked—by moralists of our time, both religious and secular. The beliefs that have led intellectuals to be content with this ignorance are not so much aristocratic as anticapitalist. Many do not wish to believe, perhaps for vaguely progressive motives, that a moral case was in fact made for the capitalist type of economy before it existed. Many intellectuals ignore the evidence of the immense benefits, in the form of prosperity, liberty, and significant moral progress, that the capitalist economies ushered into history.

I propose, therefore, briefly to rehearse the history of this decisive transformation of morals. Other writers have stressed the dazzling successes of science, industry, medicine, and technological inventiveness that have characterized capitalist societies. Moral arguments, however, play an ever larger role when humans are both free and prosperous, and therefore burdened with responsibility for making choices about what to do with their freedoms. Moreover, ours is an age in which hopes for salvation through mere economic or technological successes have come to seem illusory. It is therefore important to grasp the moral basis of the original argument for capitalism. I propose to begin with the ancient Jewish and Christian ethos regarding wealth and virtue, and then to move to the period that gradually transformed that ethos and—I would say—advanced its purposes.

This World and the Next

Irving Kristol has remarked on the difference between Jewish and Christian thinking about economics. According to Kristol, Jewish thought, whether in its prophetic or rabbinic traditions, has always felt comfortable with a certain well-ordered worldliness, whereas Christian thought has always felt a certain pull toward otherworldliness.[1] That is, Jewish thought has had a candid orientation toward private property, commercial activity, markets, and profits, whereas Christian thought—articulated from an early period chiefly by priests and monks—has persistently tried to direct the attention of its adherents beyond the activities and interests of this world to concern with the next. Tutored by the law and the prophets, ordinary Jews tend to feel more at home in this world than ordinary Christians, who are instructed to regard this world as a valley of temptation and a distraction from their proper business, which is preparation for the world to come.

To be sure, the difference between these two religious traditions is mitigated by the diaspora inflicted on the Jews two generations after the birth of Christ. The Jews of the Diaspora regard themselves as an exiled people, who in a ceremonial way look toward the future: "Next year in Jerusalem." There is an analogy between the Jewish and the Christian sense of exile. One might be tempted to see a crucial difference, in that the Jewish concern for the future has a more worldly focus than the Christian, namely, the regaining of the territory of Israel, centered in Jerusalem. However, in Jewish experience, too, the hazards of existence are such that the achievement of such aims must always be postponed—in the ultimate, until the coming of the Messiah. Until then, there is always the "not yet," and there is always a pilgrimage still to make.

The essential difference seems rather to lie in the seriousness with which Jews must take their survival and prospering in the world until the Messiah comes, whereas the Christian faith, accepting Jesus as the awaited Messiah, views this world and its striving from the perspective of eternity, which relativizes and diminishes the urgency of what happens here below in this vale of tears. This difference, too, is mitigated, however. The early Christian community eventually realized that the promised Second Coming of the Messiah was not imminent, and that Christians too would have to live in diaspora until he comes again. It became clear that they too would be required to cultivate a certain worldliness—a holy worldliness, they might hope—and a patient building up of the kingdom until the Messiah comes again. They would need an incarnational ethos. Christians had to learn to live well-ordered lives within history, much as Jews did. Both communities, each in its own way must "await the appointed hour."

Nevertheless, Christian thought is focused on eschatology (on that end-time of the entire world, "the last things") and on eternal life (that immortal participation in God's life promised to those who "eat of this bread and drink of this cup"). This focus tends to divide Christian worldly interests; Jewish interests are not divided in this way. Christians live within a different horizon from that of Jews; they see the world differently. They assign to Jesus Christ a wholly different role in history. Christians divide history into "before Christ" and "years of the Lord," not because Jesus was one of humankind's notable moral teachers, but rather because Jesus Christ is the Son of God and is the Logos, the Form in whose imitation all of creation has been created and has its being.

This Christian horizon is a mystical one. It means seeing within the world what others do not see; namely, that all things participate in God's life, lead to him, and are (as it were) fired by him as ingots are by flame. It means seeing, in addition, that the particular form of human life that Jesus lived is not only a model to be imitated, but the highest form to which human ethical striving, graced by the Creator, can attain; that is, suffering love, agape, that laying down of one's life for others in whose light all of life has been foreseen, created, and redeemed.

The ethical implication of this horizon is that Christians, insofar as they are infused with this vision, and not merely baptized, must "see" the circumstances of daily life in a unique way. They are caught in an eschatological tow (history is not merely static but moving, developing, heading toward its fruition in full participation in the life of God) and pulled upwards by a viewpoint *sub specie aeternitatis,* from whose height all worldly activities are seen to participate in the larger drama of the calling home of every human being, body and soul. Nonetheless, Christians are to be *in* the world as well as *of* the world; eschatologically drawn, but also incarnational. Properly seen, each human being is not only a soul; and Christianity is not a spiritualizing religion, in the sense of rejecting the human body. This is the crucial significance of the Incarnation, the Ascension, and even the Assumption of the Blessed Virgin Mary. As the eternal God became flesh, and in the flesh ascended into heaven, and as the first of the redeemed, his mother, was assumed body and soul to his side, so also the whole human person, body and soul, is capable of salvation. Besides its eschatological side, Christianity also has a this-worldly, bodily, incarnational side. This is the reason for the dreadful battles of the first millennium (and more) of Christian history between the orthodox community and the body-despising Gnostics, the spiritualizers, the Cathars, and others.

The Christian horizon has both an eschatological and an incarnational aspect. Christian faith is meant to be lived fully and boldly in this world, incarnationally; and also with a sense of exile, longing, and homelessness. "We have not here a lasting home." "Our hearts are restless till they rest in thee." Christians are properly at home in the flesh, in this world, and in the struggles of history to build up a kingdom of truth, justice, love, and beauty; at the same time they are pilgrims in a diaspora, in exile, and in expectation.

Monasticism and Living in the World

Judaism and Christianity are religions of history. For both, the decisive encounter in the human drama is the encounter of each human with his Creator, which issues in either "yes" or "no." The axial point of history lies in the human will. This axial point has a social as well as a personal dimension, since the Creator has entered into a social covenant with all humankind. Like Jews, Christians are constituted as a people, and the individual drama of affirmation or denial takes place in this social context.

The Creator is conceived of in terms of intellect and will: he is person, light, and truth, lover, beckoner, and promisegiver. From this vision derives the Jewish and Christian insight that humans are primarily creatures of reflection and choice, and that human history is the history of liberty. The fulcrum of existence is seen to be intellect and will: the Creator's first, and man's in imitation and response.

From this emphasis comes the vision of an ideal human society as one formed through the appeal to reason and to choice, through covenant and compact; and the sense of history as unfolding under the light of the transcendent God, a God who is undeceivable and quite demanding.[2] From such sources appears the restless drive and social dynamism of the Jewish and Christian peoples. Created in the image of their Maker, Jews and Christians have a vocation to pursue the light (to inquire), to build community (to love), and to be imaginative in changing the world (to create)—under pain of judgment.

Just the same, the Christian emphasis upon both eternal life and incarnation has complicated the task of Christian ethics. What should Christians do about the world in which they find themselves? Two tendencies, both essential and yet in considerable tension, have historically manifested themselves. The first tendency arose out of the witness to what is most original in Christianity, the eschatological vision and the call to eternal life, which inspired many of the saints, anchorites, and early monks to live as witnesses to human life as it will be lived when the Messiah returns.[3] They had as little to do with the tasks of this world as was possible in a life of union with God in prayer, contemplation, and love. They did not marry. They regarded work as a form of prayer, done solely for their own material sustenance and independence. (Some of them were partly dependent on alms.) They sought poverty in spirit, both to identify with the materially poor and to remove themselves as much as possible from worldly concerns. They surrendered their wills to God by obedience to their lawful superiors (for it is to their own wills that humans are most attached).

The irony of monastic life is, of course, that those Christian communities that first committed themselves to such unworldly and disciplined lives, such as the Benedictine and Carthusian monks of the sixth century onwards, typically reaped immense worldly success. Saint Benedict (circa A.D. 480–547) has become known as "the father of modern Europe." The Benedictine monasteries sprouting northward from Monte Cassino taught scientific farming to the wandering tribes of France and Germany; helped to lift prospering villages well above subsistence living; inspired the construction of great churches and libraries and centers of learning and the arts; taught a form of democratic governance (their abbots being elected by all in the community); inspired a respect for hours of the day and for appointed tasks in each; showed the way to a sense of international law and culture; pioneered the development of far-flung commerce and exchange; and were themselves among the first examples of independent legal corporations in Europe.[4] Conceived in poverty and detachment, the monasteries often became so rich and influential in worldly affairs as to be the envy of the covetous.

The second tendency, equally essential, was a persistent witness by Christians who continued to live in the world as others live, in all the occupations of daily life, as farmers, weavers, carpenters, stonemasons, merchants, and all the other trades. For centuries, these were mainly simple folk, serfs or peasants, who lived much as citizens of the ancient world had lived. Roads and other means of travel were few and dangerous for commerce. Worldly horizons were local. Daily living was at subsistence levels, lower in bad times, better in good, but always relatively simple. One can find many descriptions of such rural life in David Hume (1711–1776) and Adam Smith (1723–1790); ancient and medieval forms of life persisted almost universally in Europe well into the modern period.[5] The teachings of Judaism and Christianity had originally been cast in the language of people living in villages and relatively small cities; these teachings made direct and simple sense to the medieval serfs and peasants, among whom prosperity made slow headway.

Wealth in the Middle Ages

Well into the modern period, wealth was defined in one of two basic ways: either as ownership of land (and the ability to draw upon the produce of those who worked the land) or as the possession of gold, silver, precious stones, and highly crafted treasures.[6] Before roads and travel were safe, most Europeans depended on local agriculture, experiencing famine or plenty as the rhythms of nature dictated. Trade was relatively slight, and they could not rely on distant sources of sustenance. The vast majority of people lived at the level of subsistence, often precariously.

Economics seemed to be a zero-sum activity. There was little except local produce to buy. Money itself, in the form of pieces of gold, silver, or other metals, was in relatively fixed supply. Industry (such as that taught by the Benedictines) and good fortune could produce new wealth in the form of larger crops; but what could one do with these? Storage capacities were limited; spoilage was an ever-present thief. Individuals were taught to respect the place and status Providence had assigned them. There was not much social mobility.

Great landholders tended to spend their wealth on hiring retainers, raising armies, and sponsoring entertainments. The best of them, living by the feudal code of paternal care for their subjects, treated their farm laborers fairly; the worst exploited and repressed them. Large landholders owed services to the greater lords of the realm, such as supplying armies and taxes. For large landholders under conditions of feudalism (or in the ancient world, slavery), the raising of armies was both useful and easy. It was useful for conquest and pillage. It was easy because most people lived long stretches of the year in indolence; they were passive because they lacked not only the means to improve their lot but also the taste for better goods. David Hume described the situation like this:

> It is true, the ancient armies, in time of war, subsisted much upon plunder: But did not the enemy plunder in their turn? Which was a more ruinous way of levying a tax, than any other that could be devised. In short, no probable reason can be assigned for the great power of the more ancient states above the modern, but their want of commerce and luxury. Few artisans were maintained by the labour of the farmers, and therefore more soldiers might live upon it.[7]

Few people thought about the reconstruction of the social order. Anarchy and the widespread brigandage of the highways were an omnipresent threat; such order as there was, because it made sound agriculture possible, seemed to be the primary and most indispensable achievement of civilization. This civilized order was precarious. Cities were walled; palaces were fortresses.

In such a context, it was possible to regard wealth as a fragile gift of Providence, a gift that entailed responsibilities of stewardship on behalf of those passed by the hand of God into one's care. On the other hand, wealth could often be regarded as the spoils of war and as largely ill-gotten booty. Biblical texts could easily be adduced to show that wealth was not a gift but a theft. Even when it was a gift of Providence, obtained through legitimate industry or inheritance, wealth was seen as fraught with dangers to one's soul. It brought the temptation of sins against stewardship, of distraction, of inordinate worldly cares, and of ambition and covetousness.

As money came into wider use, enabling those who had it to seek out luxuries, treasures, or useful goods that were not made locally, a larger scope was given to vices such as avarice and ambition. Many goods that in modern times are commonplace were in the Middle Ages so rare that the money needed to buy them was the focal point of desire. Indolence, apathy, lust, and gluttony may have seemed to be the deadliest and most common sins in earlier days, when only local agricultural goods were available; but increasingly the possibilities of commerce and exchange shifted the forms of temptation to cupidity. The buying power of money gave a new meaning to the medieval maxim, cited by Chaucer and other writers, *Radix malorum est cupiditas:* the love of money is the root of all evil.

In a zero-sum world money acquired by one seemed to subtract from the common stock available to others. Those who measured their power by the contents of their counting houses were tempted to become misers, hoarding what they had. Misers were held in a special moral contempt, both because others could not share in their bounty and because miserliness warps the human spirit, with a peculiar narrowing down of human attention and affections. David Hume offers a discussion of avarice in this sense.[8]

In the premodern world, wealth played a rather different and far simpler role than it plays today.[9] The moral judgment to be placed on it was correspondingly simpler. In the premodern period, throughout Christendom, illness ravaged the poor. The severity of the seasons, the cycles of sterility in the soil, and many other hazards of nature caused both prolonged periods of hardship and recurrent famines. Quite often, life offered the poor considerably less than subsistence, and the average age of mortality was quite low (estimated at about eighteen years or below). A simple life just above the level of subsistence was thus considered something of a blessing. Little or no thought was given to eliminating poverty or to changing the conditions under which the poor lived. There was enormous misery, and great bands of beggars wandered about, at times breaking out in wild and furious rebellions.[10] In France near the end of the eighteenth century, 90 percent of the population lived on a very narrow diet, spending 80 percent of its income for bread alone.[11] Thomas Jefferson in the 1780s was appalled at the misery he witnessed as ambassador to France; Victor Hugo, writing of 1832, described the people of France as *Les Misérables*. Montesquieu, in effect, asked what the Christian church had done—its works of mercy aside—to alter the condition of the poor from what it had been in the time of Christ. Somewhat anachronistically, he even called the Scholastics "criminals" for their discouragement of commercial activities.[12]

The few who were wealthy lived in conspicuous luxury at the courts of the kings; great landholders built fine estates; and the cities, although nourishing a growing class of artisans, craftsmen, and merchants, were by modern standards quite humble in circumference and population. The world population at the end of the eighteenth century has been estimated at 900 million, of whom some 180 million lived in Europe.[13]

There was little cause to speak of the creation of wealth, for it was not clear to anyone that wealth could be created, at least in any systematic way. A few people were born wealthy. By industriousness, a local population or an extended family might gradually—and precariously—improve its condition. By taking great risks, a few merchants engaged in transnational commerce might become wealthy.[14] Kingdoms could grow rich by extending their dominion and enlarging their tax base; but the condition of the vast majority improved by imperceptible degrees, if at all.

There were prosperous periods and prosperous regions, but the causes of the wealth of nations had been little glimpsed—or inquired into. Politics was the first, urgent field of inquiry, not economics. It is true that the international orientation of Christendom and the Holy Roman Empire enlarged the parochial consciousness of individual rulers,[15] and that the maintenance of safe roads and the protection of trading caravans were slowly increasing the intensity of trade among the nations; nonetheless, premodern civilizations were largely agrarian, not commercial. The Franciscans and the Dominicans in Italy and France,[16] the Jesuits of Salamanca,[17] and others began to develop a theology of the laity—and therefore of commerce, prices, markets, and taxation—but this theology must be accounted premodern and precapitalist. A philosophy for a commercial civilization, let alone for an inventive, dynamic, industrial civilization, was not yet ripe for development. It had begun to blossom in the casuistry of the schools; but there did not yet exist either the broad social experience or the categories of thought that would bring it to flower.

The Modern Watershed

The glories of classical Athens appeared when Athens was only, by modern standards, a small city, built on the economic base of slavery, a very small class of men of property and civic consciousness, and (for its size) an incredibly large army which under Alexander could conquer a vast tract of the world east of Greece. David Hume wrote:

> Throughout all ancient history, it is observable, that the smallest republics raised and maintained greater armies, than states consisting of triple the number of inhabitants, are able to support at present. It is computed, that, in all European nations, the proportion between soldiers and people does not exceed one to a hundred. But we read, that the city of Rome alone, with its small territory, raised and maintained, in early times, ten legions against the Latins.[18]

Another humble and at first fairly poor region, Scotland, brought to flower during the eighteenth century a remarkable corps of intellectuals who revolutionized the way in which the world thought about wealth and virtue: such writers as David Hume, Francis Hutcheson, Adam Smith, and Thomas Reid. These were teachers of moral philosophy, with a profound interest in jurisprudence, politics, and the new science (or art) of economics. Adam Smith, the greatest of these thinkers, shared with the others a vocation to educate the rising middle class and prepare them for the world of change, the world of industry, commerce, and economic growth, which he had begun to envisage for Scotland.

By the late seventeenth century, increasing wealth through conquest had come to seem less attractive than increasing it through commerce.

> In a country not furnished with mines, there are but two ways of growing rich, either conquest or commerce. By the first the Romans made themselves masters of the riches of the world; but I think that, in our present circumstances, nobody is vain enough to entertain a thought of our reaping the profits of the world with our swords, and making the spoil and tribute of vanquished nations the fund for the supply of the charges of the government, with an overplus for the wants, and equally craving luxury, and vanity of the people.[19]

A century later, Scotland was far poorer than England, more rural, and more agrarian. It seemed to Adam Smith wise, as it had seemed earlier to John Locke and David Hume, to begin exchanging the old traditional ways of thinking about wealth and virtue for new ways. The vast majority, living in poverty, were unlikely to accept the ancient theories of virtue—those of Aristotle, Cicero, the Schoolmen, Machiavelli, and Pico della Mirandola—designed for a small elite whose privileges depended upon the labor of slaves or of the poor. Smith, like Hume, saw much to be gained by a new sort of regime, for which a new idea of virtue would be required.[20] The Scottish moralists did not so much repeal the old table of the virtues and vices as reform and revise it, so as to call to attention newly recognized moral failings and fresh moral possibilities.

The New Morality of Commerce

The first volume in Adam Smith's intended trilogy dealt with his moral vision: *The Theory of Moral Sentiments*. In his youth, Smith had studied for the Presbyterian ministry, until convinced that his true vocation lay more in the secular world, in the "higgling and bargaining" of the marketplace in a free commercial society.[21] His fundamental moral principle was that human life is relational; morality is best learned and practiced in community.[22] Smith prided himself on constructing homely examples, taken from ordinary life. He based his ethical code on the much neglected virtue of sympathy.

> And hence it is, that to feel much for others and little for ourselves, that to restrain our selfish, and to indulge our benevolent affections, constitutes the perfection of human nature; and can alone produce among mankind that harmony of sentiments and passions in which consists their whole grace and propriety. As to love our neighbour as we love ourselves is the great law of Christianity, so it is the great precept of nature to love ourselves only as we love our neighbour, or what comes to the same thing, as our neighbour is capable of loving us.[23]

The achievement of David Hume and, following him, Adam Smith, was to turn in a new direction the classic tradition on the teaching of the virtues. The classic tradition rested on the economic basis of slavery and the continued impoverishment of the poor. It ignored the life conditions of all but the civic notables, the aristocracy of honor and station, on whose shoulders pressed few onerous obligations of work, industry, or commerce. The moral life of the aristocracy was lived within a horizon of leisure shared by few others, and was guided by the distant star of noblesse oblige, far above the higgling and bargaining of daily life in the marketplace.

The ancient and medieval moralists concentrated mostly upon ends, while paying scant attention to means. Being of the nobility (economically), they could afford to concentrate on what is noble (morally). The members of this moral aristocracy saw their task as being to shape their moral consciousness by firm reflection on the true ends of life—whether the natural life or the life of faith—so as not to squander their freedom and ease on non-essentials. Meanwhile, all those of lower station than the nobility and the clergy were involved in the means of daily life: earning a living, bringing up a family, leading a civic life, and forming a social world. Hume and Smith concentrated their analyses of the moral life on these daily necessities, on the realm of means rather than of ends.

This move may be dangerous for Christian ethics, since it is essential to Christian living to keep in view the horizon of eschatology and eternal life. For a Christian, ends are extremely important, as is reflected in this famous question and answer in the Baltimore Catechism: "Why did God make me? To know Him, to love Him, and to serve Him in this world and to be happy with Him in the next." Nonetheless, practically everyone agrees that Christian social teaching even today has so far developed too little instruction for everyday living and for the higgling and bargaining of daily life. Hume and Smith perhaps say too little about ends, where Christian social teaching has been strong; on the other hand, perhaps Christian social thought has something to learn from them about means. Worth consulting, in this connection, is Alasdair MacIntyre's comparison of the moral viewpoint of Aquinas with that of modern moralists such as John Rawls.[24] However that may be, Smith is preeminent in his analysis of the new moral conditions that arise from the development of a commercial society out of an agrarian society. Hume, Smith, and others make nine distinguishable arguments in favor of the turn toward a capitalist economy.

First, life in premodern rural society was circumscribed not only by poverty but also by the absence of possibilities for self-improvement and action. The Scottish intellectuals saw such possibilities in commerce. Hume noted, for example, that economic prosperity and the virtues of liberty go together.

> Nothing tends so much to corrupt and enervate and debase the
> mind as dependency and nothing gives such noble and gener-

ous notions of probity as freedom and independency. Commerce is one great preventative of this custom. The manufacturers give the poorer sort better wages than any master can afford; besides it gives the rich an opportunity of spending their fortunes with fewer servants, which they never fail of embracing. Hence it is that the common people of England who are altogether free and independent are the honestest of their rank anywhere to be met with.[25]

Second, by ending dependency, the rise of commerce and industry would awaken the rural poor out of the slumbers of idleness. In the ancient and medieval agrarian economy, which still existed in Ireland and Scotland in the eighteenth century, Hume and Smith could see side by side the traditional rural apathy and the growing bustle and excitement of commercial living. Where manufactures and the mechanical arts are not cultivated,

> the bulk of the people must apply themselves to agriculture; and if their skill and industry increase, there must arise a great superfluity from their labour beyond what suffices to maintain them. They have no temptation, therefore, to encrease their skill and industry; since they cannot exchange that superfluity for any commodities, which may serve either to their pleasure or vanity. A habit of indolence naturally prevails. The greater part of the land lies uncultivated.[26]

The lassitude of the farm meant large numbers of men available for the call to arms, and a lack of economic development in the countryside. This was the devil's bargain struck by the nobility: a large pool of labor in exchange for continuing poverty. The factor that Hume and Smith saw would change this was the growth of manufactures, industry, and overseas commerce. These new economic activities were already introducing new goods into rural areas, awakening people to new possibilities, and offering them incentives to change their ancient ways and better their condition.

> This perhaps is the chief advantage which arises from a commerce with strangers. It rouses men from their indolence; and

presenting the gayer and more opulent part of the nation with objects of luxury, which they never before dreamed of, raises in them a desire of a more splendid way of life than what their ancestors enjoyed.[27]

What was true of the nobility was even more true of the common people: the possibility of bettering their condition would awaken them from indolence and inspire new energies. The more manufactures and commerce grew (the supply side), the larger would grow the expectations that people set for themselves (the demand side). Their economic activities would pick up, and economic growth would begin to rumble throughout the countryside from the bottom up.

Third, a commercial society is less warlike. Adam Smith pointed out that, before commerce had exercised its moderating influence, "great lords . . . [made] war continually upon one another, and very frequently upon the king; and the open country . . . [was] a scene of violence, rapine, and disorder."[28] However,

commerce and manufacture gradually introduced order and good government, and with them, the liberty and security of individuals, among the inhabitants of the country, who had before lived almost in a continual state of war with their neighbours, and of a servile dependency upon their superiors.[29]

Fourth, the practices of commerce bring people together in more frequent and more complex interactions. In a simple, physical sense, markets grow and people spend more time in markets. Village, town, and city markets become more specialized and reach farther afield.

Fifth, a commercial society would mix together the ancient social classes. It would encourage a multiplicity of voluntary associations, some of them trade based or market based, others formed for political, civic, recreational, or religious purposes.[30] Subjects would become citizens—inhabitants of cities and their surrounding regions who have a common stake in the social progress of their region and their nation. Even the number of conversations would multiply; city people are talking people. Literacy and learning would flower as incentives grew for learning about the world. The Scots, like the English, had a predisposition for conversation in taverns, pubs, and meeting halls, and in the eighteenth century, clubs of many sorts had begun to form for those interested in conversing about this or that.[31]

Sixth, as market activities grow, so also do popular knowledge, skills, and specializations. Techniques improve under competition, as new products and examples of new excellence in old products come to be known. Tastes expand. Imagination is stimulated. Markets awaken a thirst for ever more exchanges of information as people learn about the existence of new products and new techniques.

> Few merchants, who possess the secret of . . . importation and exportation, make great profits; and becoming rivals in wealth to the ancient nobility, tempt other adventurers to become their rivals in commerce. Imitation soon diffuses all those arts; while domestic manufactures emulate the foreign in their improvements, and work up every home commodity to the utmost perfection of which it is susceptible.[32]

Seventh, markets require forms of civilized behavior: patient explanation, civil manners, a willingness to be of service, and a willingness to reach satisfactory mutual consent. In this sense, wrote Adam Smith, "Commerce ought naturally to be, among nations, as among individuals, a bond of union and friendship."[33] Besides imparting new information about products, technical progress, and the larger world, markets also teach an important civilizing lesson: participants in markets should be civil, reasoned, and respectful of one another's point of view. In actuality, things do not always proceed so smoothly; but then, when more markets than one exist, the unsatisfied can always go elsewhere.

Eighth, the replacement of agrarian ways (with their relative isolation and taciturnity) by commercial ways (with their city bustle and rapid talk) tends to awaken one of the most precious, high, and rare forms of moral development: the civic need for the virtue of sympathy. Smith had a very demanding notion of what sympathy entails. We might think of it as a reflection in the circumstances of daily life in eighteenth-century Scotland on what the Christian tradition had long meant by charity. If we are not quite called to lay down our life for our neighbor, we are at least called to give him or her our full and undivided attention. Sympathy, according to Adam Smith, requires an effort of imagination greater than mere empathy or fellow feeling, and greater still than merely putting oneself in another person's shoes. Empathy is too impersonal; trying to imagine how I would feel in the other's place is too ego-centered. True sympathy entails getting out of oneself imaginatively and actually seeing and feeling the world from a perspective not one's own—not exactly as that other person happens to be seeing it, but as an ideal observer from that person's perspective might see it.[34] In this way, one would understand the world perhaps more deeply than either oneself or the other had before. This is a high ideal of civil intercourse indeed.

Ninth, pursuing this ideal helps the person of commerce to be a little more objective than others, to see a little farther, and to discern needs and possibilities that have not yet been served. Yet Smith does not finally commend sympathy solely because it is useful, but because it is good. The ideal attracted him, and he could see that it attracted his students, and his readers, as well.[35] Smith's discussion reminds one of Saint Thomas's definition of love: to will the good of another. That is, not necessarily to will what the other person happens to be willing at the moment, which may even be harmful or destructive, but to will the good as God or the ideal observer might see it. This is true love, which neither deceives nor is deceived.

The civilizing practices of markets, as well as their opening up of many possibilities for human development, attracted the moral esteem of Hume and Smith even in the period before Scotland was a highly commercial society. Hume and Smith were convinced that the commercial society represented a moral advance beyond its historical predecessors. It would inspire a new civility. It would shape a new, and superior, moral ethos. It would raise the masses of the poor out of their ancient penury, enlarge their horizons and possibilities, and teach all social classes new ways of conducting themselves in social interchange.

Interests versus Passions

A reader of traditional treatises on ethics will note that Hume and Smith are concerned with sentiments rather than virtues, reversing the emphasis of the classical texts. There is a danger in concerning oneself with sentiments; one may slip over into consulting unreliable, untutored, and even unworthy feelings rather than the quiet voice of reason, duty, and responsibility. To follow one's feelings is often no liberation, but a form of slavery. Some have tried to ascribe this penchant for sentiment among British moralists to the fact that the sentiments of the British people, in the eighteenth century at least, were different from those of other cultures: more commonsensical, steady, honest, and civil. Such solid characteristics, in any case, were the ones of which Hume and Smith approved. In their defense, it may be argued that Aristotle himself seems to be making an analogous point in those passages in which he talks about education, toward the end of the *Nicomachean Ethics*. He writes of the blessing those children receive who have learned to feel pleasure and pain for the right things, and whose feelings have been tutored in ways conducive to the right ordering inherent in practical wisdom.[36] Perhaps the British emphasis on practicality led Hume, Smith, and others to begin their ethical reflections where Aristotle left off, with the education of the sentiments.

There is also a deeper reason. One of the great destroyers of societies is untamed passion. The seven deadly sins all spring from errant passion: pride, lust, envy, anger, avarice, gluttony, and sloth. Any society that would be virtuous must quiet these passions; it must displace them from the center of social dynamics. In the early stages of the Renaissance in Italy, and later throughout Europe, local princes became locked in deadly struggles to advance their power and their fame. The new morality of power and uninhibited passion was described and celebrated by Niccolò Machiavelli. The law of God and the natural law articulated by

Roman statesmen such as Cicero gave way to the autonomy of power and passion. Indeed, the meaning of the expression "natural law" shifted in Machiavelli from those activities that men ought to perform or to avoid in order to fulfill the possibilities of their rational nature, to those activities that were necessary to the designs of great men seeking fame and power. To be obedient to the natural law no longer meant meeting the demands of human (and Christian) virtue, but rather following the existing and often barbarous laws of survival and the will to power. Life came to be seen as a war, and great men were almost without exception expected to be warriors (or artists who celebrated them). Even the Vatican, being captured in those days by rival aristocracies of power, was often caught up in practice with this new moral reality, as Machiavelli chronicled.

Great passions for glory, fame, power, and self-assertion proved to be immensely destructive. Moral and political anarchy spread; and religion itself, once Europe became religiously divided, was at times the motive, or at least the cover, for the ambition of princes. The age of heroes and of grand passions erupted in prolonged political and religious wars. The ethos of the natural law and God's law had yielded to the ethos of the great passions, and the new tree bore the bitter fruit of plunder, rapine, and war.

On what basis, then, could a better morality be built? How could the great passions be tamed? How could human energy be shifted toward constructive, rather than destructive, aims? This was the problem that, especially in England and Scotland, moral philosophers set out to solve.

By shifting the moral ethos from the passions of the great to the sounder sentiments of ordinary people, such writers as David Hume and Adam Smith sought to construct a new ethos for Western civilization and, indeed, the world. They did not deny the power of passions such as pride, ambition, bellicosity, and the lust for power. Rather, they attempted to provide for these passions a new focal point: the development of wealth from commerce and industry. They argued that the powerful and the passionate could obtain in an orderly way the very fruits that they had been seeking through anarchic and warlike means. Commerce and industry would yield them an abundance and material comfort far beyond their present rough and often harsh daily circumstances, while simultaneously energizing and empowering the large populations of the rural poor. It would require peace rather than war, and it would require respect for law; only under these conditions could long-term commercial and industrial contracts be carried out and international commerce raise the standard of living for everyone.

In his penetrating but flawed book *The Passions and the Interests: Political Arguments for Capitalism before Its Triumph,* Albert O. Hirschman has tried to discern the lineaments of this shift within the European (and especially the British and French) ethos.[37] Hirschman begins by confronting a fundamental problem: How did it happen that the desire for money (*cupiditas*), hitherto considered a great sin (and even "the root of all evil"), came to be accepted in European social life, and by the end of the eighteenth century, even to be advanced by prominent moralists as a great step forward for social morality? Hirschman argues that this transformation occurred in three steps.

The first step was the debunking of the earlier religious and philosophic tradition—the tradition of natural law—as ineffectual; that is, as unable either to describe how men actually behaved or to control the destructive passions. In this step is implied a decline of the ethos of the passions, which had been discredited by its manifest destructiveness.

The second step occurred when moralists began to argue that one set of passions, those concerned with money making, can be made to counter and to check the more destructive set of passions. "A man," Samuel Johnson remarked, "is seldom so innocently engaged as in the getting of money." It was argued, by Montesquieu, for example, that commerce tames the rude and destructive passions and encourages the more humble passions such as prudence and contentment with small but steady gains—which can accrue into very great gains indeed, and for whole nations, not solely for a few aristocrats. The middle classes, whose locus of activity was the town and the city, were seen to be the carriers of new, humane values and the heroic aristocracy was lowered in the moral calculus.

71

The third step was a shift of the focus of moral analysis, from passions to interests. In Hirschman's interpretation, the interests, even the primary interest of bettering one's material condition, were seen as imposing on the passions a degree of rationality and stability. Interests would tame the passions and make them politically safe. This conception "took the form of opposing the *interests* of men to their *passions,* and of contrasting the favorable effects that follow when men are guided by their interests with the calamitous state of affairs that prevails when men give free rein to their passions."[38]

Hirschman argues that the concept of interest was increasingly narrowed down to purely material and economic interests. He errs, I think, in not making a sufficient distinction here between the British Enlightenment and that of the Continent. There is no question that material and economic interests came to assume an ever larger role for those who thought about politics. "Plenty" came to rival "power" as a political objective in the minds of political thinkers and statesmen in the seventeenth and eighteenth centuries;[39] and the first was seen to be a precondition of the second. Thus, a decisive text for Hirschman is Adam Smith's classic formulation of the overriding motive of man: "An augmentation of fortune is the *means* by which the greater part of men propose and wish to better their condition. It is the *means* the most vulgar and the most obvious."[40] Hirschman interprets this text as a narrowing down of the ample term "interests" to sheerly material purposes. Yet Smith's text shows, as do many texts in Hume, that British moralists went far beyond material purposes in their conception of interests: they saw the augmentation of fortune as a means, not an end. By contrast, the more heroic traditions lingered on in the cultures of the Continent, where considerable contempt was expressed by poets and philosophers for mere material interests. Schiller, for example, exclaims in a lament, quoted by Hirschman, "For the world is ruled only by interest."[41]

One cannot read the essays of Hume without discerning their moral force. In addition, he led a life much admired by those who knew him well.[42] One cannot confine him in the narrow, pinched vision that Hirschman appears to put forward. Nor can one read Smith's *Theory of Moral Sentiments,* or parallel passages in *The*

Wealth of Nations, without discerning that Smith held material interests as but a means to the good life. The perfection of human sentiments in a full and disinterested sympathy was for Smith (and for British moralists generally) the highest form of life.

Hume, Smith, and other British moralists saw a regime anchored in commerce and the political objective of producing plenty, as an improvement of human social life beyond the calamitous circumstances of all previous regimes. Hirschman himself retains, however, a sort of continental, aristocratic disdain for such a regime. He does not recognize that Hume and Smith use such words as "avarice" and "acquisitiveness" in two differing senses. As Hume's aforementioned essay on avarice demonstrates, such words were sometimes given a negative meaning, with connotations of miserliness, graspingness, and self-centeredness, especially in discussions of regimes of scarcity and narrow horizons. Hume and Smith use the words "avarice" and "acquisitiveness" with a positive connotation, however, when they are contrasting vitality to slumber, desire to lassitude, and ambition to idleness. The drive to better one's condition is not evil but good; even professors of intellectual history need not be ashamed to share in it. There is a good "avarice" and bad.

It is characteristic of self-consciously revolutionary thinkers, such as Hume and Smith, that they can scarcely resist turning the highly charged meanings of the established order on their head, in order to transvalue them. What earlier moralists had considered "the most vulgar and the most obvious," Smith was explicitly willing to make the humble foundation of his system. He thus dared traditionalists to argue that it is wrong for ordinary people trapped in mean circumstances "to propose and to wish the bettering of their condition." If a greater material comfort is seen by "the great part of men" as a means of bettering their condition, it does not follow that such comfort is the full and final end of what they wish to achieve.

One of the untold stories of capitalist development—a story resisted by traditionalists and socialists alike—would display the broad-minded and humane concerns that such development inspired in the growing middle class, who awakened national concern for the deplorable state of the poor, *les misérables.* The plight of the poor was a main concern of Hume and Smith. They attacked the moral standing of traditionalists by asking what their regimes had done for the vast masses of the poor on whom traditional regimes rested, and who were recruited as soldiers in pursuit of those regimes' destructive passions.

In arguing for capitalism before its triumph, Hume and Smith also had in mind the surge of spiritual independence and the extension of humane sympathies that would flow from the sway of a more free and beneficent regime. Smith saw his life's work as becoming a moral teacher for the new class of jurists, entrepreneurs, industrialists, merchants, bankers, and civil servants, whose numerical growth he was championing in Scotland and, by implication, in all nations.[43] From this large-minded conception of the capitalist ethos there flowed the multitudes of sympathetic studies on which Engels drew (for antagonistic purposes) in his *The Condition of the Working Class in England;* there flowed steady advances in the care of all the ailments to which common people are prey; and there flowed freedom of the press, an emphasis upon education for the new industrial workers, and a general pattern of upward social and cultural striving. Hirschman writes as if to demean the bourgeois revolution by interpreting it in the narrowest way possible. He fails to see the humane grandeur of its purposes and its historical achievements.

The Bourgeois Revolution

What Hirschman leaves out of his analysis, the contemporary world has not failed to see. It has turned out that the citizens of Estonia, Latvia, and Lithuania, of Poland and Hungary, and even of Russia and China, do seem "to propose and to wish to better their condition"—and so, it seems, do virtually all the peoples of the world. Most vulgar and most obvious this basic wish may seem and yet, amazingly, quantities of ink (not to mention blood) have been spilled by the past century's ideologues to repress it or to disguise it. The artists, scholars, and intellectuals of the West seem unaccountably ashamed to be implicated in promoting its fulfillment. A recent cartoon by Jules Feiffer catches this treason of the clerks succinctly. A black-garbed, bearded artist, brush in hand, cries out in successive panels:

> My art exposes your commercialism . . .
> your overindulgence—materialism . . .
> acquisitiveness . . .
> your greed, your narcissism . . .
> your corrupt ethics—morality . . . .
> I dedicate my life as an artist to the free
> expression of my contempt for what you are . . . .
> Fund me.[44]

Confronted by a planet on which the vast majority of their fellow humans live in conditions too appalling to countenance, what do these enemies of capitalism, even now after its triumph, propose to offer? The stone of socialism? The scandal of traditional precapitalist economies ruled by the passions of caudillos and tribal chiefs?

Since the bold theorists of the seventeenth and eighteenth centuries humanely sketched them out, the full moral resources of the capitalist revolution have never yet been plumbed. This may be due to the downward mobility in status of all aristocracies, including that of artists and intellectuals, who traditionally have celebrated the aristocracy while making the bourgeoisie their sworn enemy. Artists and intellectuals have shown almost universal contempt for the bourgeoisie and their commerce and their industry—and for their manifold and obvious virtues even more than for their often glaring (and self-admitted) faults. I doubt if any leading class in history has more patiently borne, and more self-critically enjoyed, the mockery that artists have heaped upon them; they have even paid for that mockery.

Behind the bourgeois ethos lies a deep web of traditional assumptions: that all human beings are of one interdependent family; that all experience upward strivings, both material and spiritual; that a precondition of self-governance and of life under regimes formed by the consent of the governed is an economy of openness and plenty; that the rights of minorities—individual rights, even—are as deserving of the protection of governments as is the public good; that human rights are, in practice, best protected under conditions of economic independence for the many, with checks and balances against political ambition; that the pursuit of plenty, although an indispensable means to humankind's flourishing, is not an end in itself; that freedom is not solely freedom from want and tyranny, but also the exercise of ancient virtues such as honesty, courage, justice, and sober temperance; and that only the exercise of these virtues enables men and women to use their full capacity for human liberty.

The bourgeois revolution is no mean and petty thing. From often brutal experience, citizens around the world have come to discern quite clearly the illusions of salvation through politics, and the boredom-inducing limits of mere economism. In its present stage the bourgeois revolution has opened up before us the realm of moral and cultural development. True moral primacy lies, now as ever, in the groping sense among hundreds of millions of economically liberated persons that plenty is only a means, and that the true vocation of free peoples lies in the development of those inner strengths that give acts of liberty their beauty: those practices of sobriety, justice, and generosity that our nature commands. Without these practices, humans have missed the point of liberty.

By contrast with the pursuit of power, glory, and passion, the systematic pursuit of wealth constitutes a fundamental improvement in the human understanding of the path toward virtue. This improvement, however, is only the threshold. We must step over it to confront our most urgent and broadly perceived social worry today: the disorder and missed possibilities of our moral lives. Hume, Smith, and others correctly perceived wealth to be a useful means for opening up to all, and not merely to aristocrats, the pursuit of virtue. Now the vista they opened up—self-education in moral virtue—lies before us. The world's peoples seem to sense this, and to express an almost universal disaffection with the merely economic and political salvation myths that have devastated the modern world.

"The revolution," the poet Charles Peguy said, "is moral or not at all."

The Future Task for Religious Ethics

It follows from this brief survey of the eighteenth-century Scottish revolution in ethical thinking that the teaching of Christians and Jews need not, with respect to economics, begin from scratch. In the precapitalist world of almost universal poverty, a world that gave little thought to the systematic creation of wealth, it may have been understandable to focus ethical reflection chiefly upon remedies for misery. For some, it remains a great temptation to continue such precapitalist modes of thinking even today. The dream of socialism, rooted in the flawed economic doctrines of the nineteenth century, has heightened that temptation. That dream ended in the last part of the twentieth century in a night-mare—in China, in the Soviet Union, in Eastern Europe, and in all the other Marxist nations.

We read, for example, of unbelievable shortages of soap, medicines, and other basic items of everyday living in Poland and the USSR. Shelves in stores are empty. Basic foods are scarce. Dental care proceeds without anesthetics. Such goods as are pro-duced are of inferior quality, and sometimes hardly usable. "If you socialized the Sahara," a mordant Eastern European saying goes, "in two years there would be a shortage of sand."

According to a detailed report by Zbigniew Bochniarz of the University of Minnesota's Hubert Humphrey Institute:

> 27 areas containing a third of Poland's population are regarded as "ecological hazards" due to multiple violations of standards. Norms are consistently exceeded at 60% of nitrogen oxide monitoring sites and 80% of those for dust and soot emissions. Four-fifths of Poland's soils have become highly acidified; 70% of its southern forests are projected to die by century's end. Be-tween 1965 and 1985, Polish waters fit for human consumption dropped from 33% to 6% of all surface waters, while those unfit even for industry use nearly doubled.

Poland produces about 20 times more soot and five times more sulfur dioxide and solid waste per unit of gross national product than does Western Europe. Its mortality rate for males over 35 is about 50% higher than West Germany's, and 50% higher in hazard areas than the national average. Since 1978, average annual growth rates for most pollutants have outstripped the growth of GNP.[45]

Meanwhile, even in the democratic and capitalist countries, men and women of enterprise work without the moral and intellectual support of thinkers and moralists. A capitalist system has come into being, but its moral purposes are left inarticulate. Serious Jews and Christians, asking for moral guidance in their wealth-creating activities, encounter silence, if not rejection. Men and women of enterprise know that they are doing something valuable, but their efforts go without recognition, moral support, or ethical guidance.

The nine moral arguments in favor of creative economies, discussed in this chapter, have already been dimly grasped even in the citadels of socialist society, in Hungary and Poland, in the Soviet Union, and among scholars in China. They are, however, seldom reflected upon, and made into guideposts, in the West.

These nine arguments have a profound relationship to Jewish and Christian theology. God created humans in his image; that is, to become creators. In the Jewish and Christian vision, human beings are born free and responsible. They have inalienable rights to life, liberty and, as Pope John Paul II has recently emphasized, enterprise.[46] The existing systems of political economy need to be restructured so as to be worthy of these images of God. There is still vast poverty, and the needs of this earth's ever larger population continue to grow. There is clearly a need for a full-fledged ethic of wealth production, for economic systems designed to encourage such production, and for the practices and habits that allow it to take place and that make it humane.

To be sure, the "augmentation of fortune" is only a means; but it is a necessary means. Like every other human activity, it is subject to corruption and misuse, and those abuses must be guarded against. The best moral instruction, however, begins by raising aloft the ideal to be pursued: the exercise of God-given talents to imagine, invent, discover, and bring into widespread use the resources that God has hidden in the natural world. To develop in all humans the virtue of enterprise, so that they might exercise their creative capacities, is a task that, especially in the third world, is far from accomplished. Institutional supports for this creativity need to be imagined, experimented with, and made to work. These include accessible, quick, and inexpensive institutions for incorporating new businesses; institutions of credit, especially for the poor; markets open to the poor; an education in the moral and intellectual virtues of enterprise; and the transmission of skills in every field of economic creativity. No society ought to depend on only a relatively small economic elite; all citizens, especially the poor, should be brought into participation in enterprising, wealth-creating activities, and all those other creative endeavors that make the environment of work humane.[47] Every man and woman has a fundamental right to engage in personal economic enterprise. Existing systems should be scrutinized in the light of how they assist, or block, the exercise of that right.

Humans were not created to be receivers only, or clients only, but also creators. God gave them minds and imaginations, as well as courage and a zest for trial and error. He implanted in them a desire to better their condition, for their families and for the whole of human society. The creation of wealth is a social task and the supportive efforts of all are necessary to its accomplishment. It is especially necessary for the poor. We now know that wealth can be created in a sustained and systematic way; therefore—given the immense suffering of so many poor—economic development has become a moral obligation. We are obliged to shape institutions and systems that permit its flourishing.

Both the traditionalist and the socialist economic visions have proved to be inadequate. The capacity of capitalist and democratic systems to improve the living conditions of hundreds of millions of the poor has been abundantly proved. Such systems do not promise, or deliver, paradise on earth; they are but instruments of our larger moral and cultural purposes. But it is precisely the moral and

79

cultural leaders of the free societies who have been most deficient in grasping the moral and spiritual possibilities that these novel systems of political economy have opened up before us. The thinkers of the Scottish Enlightenment achieved a revolution in the human ethos, a revolution whose spiritual possibilities have yet to be realized. It is my hope that moral and cultural leaders, philosophers and poets, theologians and prelates, will grasp these possibilities, and fashion from them the maxims of practical moral guidance for which so many economic activists are manifestly thirsty.

Camels and Needles, Talents and Treasure: American Catholicism and the Capitalist Ethic

Where your treasure is, there will your heart be also.

Matthew 6:21

And Jesus said to his disciples, "Truly, I say to you, it will be hard for a rich man to enter the kingdom of heaven. Again I tell you, it is easier for a camel to pass through the eye of a needle than for a rich man to enter the kingdom of God." When the disciples heard this they were greatly astonished, saying, "Who then can be saved?" But Jesus looked at them and said to them, "With men it is impossible, but with God all things are possible."

Matthew 19:23–26

[The kingdom of heaven] will be as when a man going on a journey called his servants and entrusted to them his property; to one he gave five talents, to another two, to another one, according to his ability. Then he went away. He who had received the five talents went at once and traded with them; and he made five talents more. . . . But he who had received the one talent went and dug in the ground and hid his

81

master's money. Now after a long time the master of those servants came and settled accounts with them. And he who had received the five talents came forward, bringing five talents more, saying, "Master, you delivered to me five talents; here I have made five talents more." His master said to him, "Well done, good and faithful servant; you have been faithful over a little, I will set you over much more; enter into the joy of your master." . . . He also who had received the one talent came forward, saying, "Master, I knew you to be a hard man . . . so I was afraid, and I went and hid your talent in the ground. Here is what is yours." But his master answered him, "You wicked and slothful servant! You knew that I reap where I have not sowed, and gathered where I have not winnowed? Then you ought to have invested my money with the bankers, and at my coming I should have received what was my own with interest. . . . Cast the worthless servant into the outer darkness; there men will weep and gnash their teeth."

Matthew 25:14–30

Imagine yourself a successful, contemporary American Catholic businessperson. You have achieved a level of material prosperity of which your grandparents (who were probably immigrants) could only dream. Your faith, which you take seriously (probably far more seriously than your WASP or Jewish colleagues, although perhaps less intensely than your evangelical Protestant fellow entrepreneurs), is not an obstruction to your economic or social success and status, as it might have been a generation ago; on the contrary, you are regularly struck by the number of fellow Catholics whom you meet at the higher altitudes of CEO-dom. Your regular donations to the church and your secular charitable and philanthropic activities seem to be morally and spiritually legitimated by what you hear from the pulpit in your suburban parish on Sunday, and in the pastoral letters (and annual drive requests!) of your bishop. The occasional glance at the *National Catholic Reporter* notwithstanding, you do not feel any serious tension between your way of life (and in particular your economic and social status) and your Catholic commitment.

But what about your daily activities? Do you hear or read any-thing from the formal religious leadership of the church that could be construed as a moral, theological, and spiritual legitima-tion of your efforts to create wealth? Your entrepreneurial energies have made jobs available to others. Your success has meant suc-cess—in investments, in employment, in personal satisfaction—for thousands of your employees and shareholders. Through the tax system, and through your philanthropic activities, you are making a significant contribution to the common good. What does your Catholicism have to say about all that?

If the truth be told, it probably doesn't have much to say at all. And if a further truth be told, that fact probably doesn't worry you very much. It does concern the contributors to this book, though, and eventually it may well concern you (it will certainly concern your children). Why does an ancient religious tradition, successfully inculturated in the United States and claiming that its social teach-ing and its various approaches to lay spirituality carry insights into the public dimension of human life, seem to have so little to say to you and others like you in terms of the activities that dominate your professional life? Is there something in the nature of Catholic social thought, as it has evolved over the past century, that impedes the development of an ethic of wealth creation? How have the special historical and sociological circumstances of Catholicism in the United States contributed to today's situation? Are there resources in the Catholic tradition, in its classical expressions as well as in its distinctively American experience, that might lend themselves to the development of an ethic of entrepreneurship and wealth cre-ation, and to the definition of a lay spirituality for a society primar-ily characterized by abundance rather than poverty?

One might well argue that the first of these questions is not entirely fair: did the sociological conditions for the possibility of an ethic of wealth creation exist in American Catholicism before, say, the late 1950s? Still, given the massive empirical evidence that Cath-olics have, in the main, achieved success in the United States, one might think that this achievement would have been sustained in part by a theology, ethics, and spirituality that gave moral legiti-mation to American Catholics' drive for economic success. Indeed, the very fact of Catholic success suggests that there was nothing in the popular spirituality of American Catholicism before the Second Vatican Council that impeded Catholic economic energies. On the contrary, the church's traditional emphasis on education, its legitimation of the bourgeois family, its stress on personal discipline (in the order of ideas and values), and its sundry formal and informal networks and support systems (in the order of institutions), undoubtedly played a significant and positive role in the assimilation and economic success of the American Catholic community. It would be going too far, however, to suggest that this popular spirituality was buttressed by a theological and ethical rationale that could plausibly be termed an ethic of wealth creation. Still less would it be true to say that contemporary American Catholicism's formal religious leadership and intellectual elites seem to feel an urgency about the development of such an ethic today. A brief review of some salient episodes in American Catholic history may help explain these two distinct, but related, phenomena.

Not Quite Ready for Prime Time

In 1776 there were but 35,000 or so Catholics in the newly proclaimed United States (0.8 percent of the national population); they lived primarily in Maryland, with enclaves in New York, Pennsylvania, and the French settlements west of the Alleghenies. The leadership of this tiny community (whose members, at the time of the revolution, were still legally disenfranchised in Maryland, the colony founded in 1634 as a religious refuge for them) was firmly in the hands of "old Catholics" from the Maryland gentry, such as the Carroll family, whose two most prominent members, John Carroll and Charles Carroll of Carrollton, were, respectively, the first Catholic bishop in the United States and the last surviving signer of the Declaration of Independence. At his death in 1832, Charles Carroll of Carrollton was also reputed to be the wealthiest individual in the United States.

Archbishop John Carroll's impressive efforts to bring some order and stability to Catholic life in the United States, and

Charles Carroll's work (often in tandem with his episcopal cousin) to break through the barriers of anti-Catholic prejudice that continued to exist even after the revolution, are beyond the scope of this chapter.[1] What we should remember is that this brief hegemony of the Maryland-centered old Catholics—a gentry class whose spirituality was largely ordered to private devotion (given the paucity of clergy to lead public worship, and the dangers attendant thereon due to anti-Catholic bigotry)[2]—were quickly displaced by the waves of immigration that, beginning in the early nineteenth century, soon engulfed and transformed the American Catholic community.

These new Catholic Americans, primarily Irish, were indeed the "wretched refuse" of the Old World. Desperately poor, usually illiterate, lacking the work skills and personal disciplines that were important elements of success in the early stages of the Industrial Revolution, the immigrants of the antebellum nineteenth century were a challenge to the church of extraordinary proportions. That the challenge was, in the main, successfully met—that the laboring class in the United States was not lost to the church as it was in Europe at that very time—remains one of the crowning glories of Catholicism in the United States. It must be conceded, however, that these were not the circumstances in which the development of a sophisticated ethic of wealth creation, or a spirituality of entrepreneurship, was likely. When it occasionally turned its attention beyond the neighborhood parish to the wider national economic and social scene, a working-class church—and particularly a church led, in the 1840s and 1850s, by men like Archbishop "Dagger John" Hughes of New York—would naturally reflect the concerns, anxieties, and perspectives of its constituents.

Archbishop Hughes was a pugnacious Irish immigrant,[3] and thus perhaps a suspect witness in matters related to perfidious Albion. Nevertheless, his lurid description of conditions in English society in 1844, in what he freely conceded was the richest country in the world, gives us some of the flavor (and argumentation) of antebellum American Catholic social thought, as well as an insight into the kind of modernity that Hughes (and doubtless other American Catholic leaders) wished to avoid in America:

[England] has, indeed, fought the great battle for wealth with other countries and has, by universal consent, gained the victory. But how comes it that, while a few of her sons are rioting in the spoils of the vanquished, the cries of the wounded and dying of her own battalions, are heard on every side? How comes it that in Ireland, out of a population between eight and nine millions, there are over two millions absolutely dependent on the charity of others, scarcely a degree above their own condition? How comes it that, in Scotland, misery and destitution are hardly less general, and, from other causes, perhaps even more excruciating still? How comes it that, in England itself, distress among the laboring classes presses, at intervals, to such an extreme point, as to threaten, from time to time, insurrection and revolution? How comes it, in fine, to happen that, while the dogs of landlords and capitalists are well fed and well housed—while their horses are daintily provided for, the sons and daughters of Britons around them go forth with gaunt looks and sunken features, through want of food? These are results which *puzzle* political economists, but which never could have happened, if Political Economy had not been transferred from the Christian basis on which it was originally reared in that country, to the inadequate foundations of mere individual interest. I am willing, then, to ascribe to the Protestant religion, the credit of England's wealth; but her poverty, and the destitution of her millions, must, I insist upon it, be charged to the same account.[4]

Hughes's lecture reflected several prominent themes in antebellum American Catholic social thought: its romanticizing of the socioeconomic circumstances of the Middle Ages; its identification (which Hughes adopted from William Cobbett) of capitalism with Protestantism and, through Protestantism, with a radical individualism; its linkage of the profit motive to greed and selfishness; its view that Protestantism had destroyed the traditional authorities of the *ancien régime,* which had instructed people on their charitable duties; and its insistence on Catholicism as the only possible foundation of a just and humane society ordered to the common good.

Hughes's concerns were shared by the lay intellectual Orestes Brownson, whose 1840 polemic against capitalism was, if anything, more strident than the archbishop's. Brownson inveighed against what he took to be the moral hypocrisies of his age: "The owner who is involved in the systematic exploitation of . . . poor laborers is frequently one of our respectable citizens; perhaps he is praised in the newspapers for his liberal donations to some charitable institution. He passes among us as a pattern of morality, and is honored as a worthy Christian."[5] These hypocrisies were the inevitable result of the class antagonisms that were endemic to capitalism: "It is for the interest of the trader to cheat—to buy under value and to sell over value; it is for the interest of the master to oppress the workman, by paying the least possible wages for the least [sic] possible amount of labor. Thus is the interest of one opposed to the interest of the other; and every man in pursuing his own interest must needs, as far as possible, overreach and supplant every other man."[6] The root of the evils of capitalism lay in the wage system: "Wages is a cunning device of the devil, for the benefit of tender consciences who would retain all the advantages of the slave system, without the experience, trouble, and odium of being slave-holders."[7] Contrary to the claims of its nineteenth-century advocates, capitalism had made things worse rather than better: "The actual condition of the workingman today, viewed in all its bearings, is not so good as it was fifty years ago."[8]

Brownson shared Hughes's fondness for the Middle Ages (in which, he argued, there was less class antagonism than in antebellum America[9]), but he did not advocate a return to medieval social and economic patterns as such. Rather, "Brownson anticipated a reconstructed social order where the division between morality and politics and religion and economics was overcome in favor of a society where cooperation between brothers and sisters in pursuit of a common destiny was reflected in the halls of government and in the work places of America."[10] However, as the admiring John Mitchell delicately put it, "Brownson was unwilling to offer a detailed plan" for how this idealized and re-Christianized society might be constructed.[11]

There is nothing terribly original in Hughes's or Brownson's critiques; Hughes drew on Cobbett, and Brownson on Thomas Carlyle, for their portraits of working-class life and for their analyses of the causes of poverty. We should note, however, the antimodernity strand in both Hughes and Brownson, and their seeming fondness for a monistic approach to questions of religion and society. Was the animus of Hughes and Brownson against capitalism per se, or against capitalism as the economic expression of modernization? And was this antimodernity polemic fueled by an instinctive preference for a more intimate linkage between the church and the society, the economy, and the polity—for monism rather than pluralism in the construction of the public order?

In any event, Hughes's and Brownson's war against capitalism—the sensibility that informed their critiques, the sociological situation from which they arose, the terms in which they were expressed, the alternative models they seemed to favor—suggests that American Catholicism was in no little condition to develop an ethic of wealth creation in the mid-nineteenth century. Distribution, or, more accurately, maldistribution of wealth, was the primary concern of the leaders of antebellum American Catholicism when they turned their minds to matters economic.

After the Civil War, the most sustained ideological interaction between the formal leadership of the church and the American economic system was on the question of trade unionism. Other issues, and some large-scale personalities, were also in play, complicating the picture in this period: these were the days in which Father Edward McGlynn was excommunicated for his advocacy of the economic and tax theories of Henry George;[12] at just about the same time, Archbishop John Ireland had his new seminary in St. Paul built by the robber baron James J. Hill.[13] However, the issue that would have a decisive influence on the social thought of American Catholicism was trade unionism.

Archbishop Ireland's relationship with Hill, Cardinal James Gibbons's happy friendships with the leading families of Baltimore, and similar patterns of behavior on the part of other major American Catholic leaders suggest that the late-nineteenth-century leadership of the church was neither hostile to capitalism per se nor to capitalists as individuals. Given their primarily working-class constituency, however, and their determination that the debacle of European Catholicism in its loss of the working class not be repeated in the New World, it was only natural that the bishops' attention be focused in the first instance on workers rather than on entrepreneurs, on labor rather than on capital.

The case that brought the labor issue to a head was the attempt, generated by conservative French Canadian bishops (with some help from members of the U.S. hierarchy in whose dioceses there had been violent strikes), to get the Vatican to condemn the Knights of Labor, a forerunner of modern trade union federations. The Knights case was complicated by the organization's secrecy provisions (which were necessary for its functioning in those nasty days, but which, to Roman eyes, smacked of such condemned secret societies as the Masons), and by some of its leaders' support for Father McGlynn. To make a long and complex story drastically short,[14] the personal intervention of Cardinal Gibbons in Rome in 1887 prevented a Holy Office condemnation of the Knights, whose leadership at that time included a number of Catholics. (Interestingly enough, the Holy Office document allowing that the Knights could be "tolerated" also required that, in their constitution, "words which seem to favor socialism and communism must be amended in such a way as to make clear that the soil was granted by God to man, or rather the human race, that each one might have the right to acquire some portion of it, by use however of lawful means and without violation of the right of private property."[15])

Gibbons's intervention in the Knights of Labor controversy established a pattern of support between the American hierarchy and the American trade union movement that continues to this day—a pattern that, although not quite precluding the development of an ethic of wealth creation, mitigated against it because of a primary focus on issues of wealth distribution. One of the high points of the church-labor connection was the 1919 Bishops' Program for Social Reconstruction, issued in the wake of World War I. The program's proposals, which were condemned by the National Association of Manufacturers as "partisan, pro-labor union, socialistic propaganda,"[16] became the agenda of the National Catholic Welfare Conference's social action department during the interwar period. Gerald Fogarty summarizes the Bishops' Program, the brainchild of Catholic University's professor of moral theology, Father John A. Ryan, in these terms:

> It called on the government to retain certain wartime agencies, notably the United States Employment Service and the National War Labor Board, which supported the rights to a living wage, to organized labor, and to collective bargaining. It asked for government loans to returning servicemen, for prevention of monopolies in commodities, for government regulation of monopolies of privately owned public services, and for heavy taxation of incomes and inheritances. It went on to propose government competition with private industry if anti-trust laws failed, wider distribution of stock among employees, the elimination of child labor through government taxation, and, while not favoring women in the labor force, equal pay for equal work for both men and women.[17]

Reactions to the Bishops' Program were divided along ideological lines. Raymond Swing, writing in the *Nation,* thought that Father Ryan had produced something "better than anything produced by the AFL."[18] Conversely, a New York state senate committee investigating sedition claimed that the document came from "a certain group in the Catholic Church with leanings toward Socialism."[19] Much of this ideological cannonading became muted, of course, when the key provisions of the 1919 program were written into law during Franklin Roosevelt's first administration (a development that earned Father [later Monsignor] Ryan the sobriquet "Right Reverend New Dealer"). For our purposes, however, the Bishops' Program is important as another signal that the times were not precisely right for the development of an ethic of wealth creation in American Catholicism. The focus remained, through the Great Depression and World War II, on the ethics of distribution, not creation.

The same focus is apparent in the Roman documents of the same period. Although Dennis McCann is indulging in hyperbole when he characterizes Pope Leo XIII, author of *Rerum Novarum,* the Magna Carta of modern Catholic social thought, as "a dispossessed Italian prince unable to come to terms with the final disappearance of a feudal, agrarian society even in Central Europe,"[20] it is certainly true that *Rerum Novarum* was no radical document. Its endorsement of trade unionism was perhaps its most progressive feature, but the encyclical also went to great lengths to defend the rights of private property against socialism and communism, which Leo XIII seemed to find more immediately threatening than capitalism. On the other hand, McCann is surely right that Leo held no brief for "the capitalist ethic," and would probably have regarded the term as oxymoronic. Official Roman nervousness about capitalism (which, again, is not altogether easy to disentangle from official Roman nervousness about modernization in general during this period) is also evident in the great social encyclical of Pius XI, *Quadragesimo Anno* (1931), whose corporatism was proposed as a "third way" between capitalism and communism. Not unlike that of Hughes and Brownson, official Roman social teaching found both the market and the commissars deficient in religious and moral grounding, and seemed to regard this deficiency as an inherent one in both instances. Here, too, was unfertile soil on which to expect an ethic of wealth creation to develop.

The Catholic discussion of political economy was complexified by the Second Vatican Council, whose tripartite discussion of modern society in *Gaudium et Spes* (the 1965 "Pastoral Constitution on the Church in the Modern World") anticipated later commentators' analysis of "democratic capitalism" as a system involving a market-oriented economy, a liberal democratic polity, and a pluralistic culture.[21] However, the council's economics again stressed issues of distribution over issues of wealth creation; paid far more attention to labor than to entrepreneurship; and analyzed the difficulties of the third world in terms of what the council fathers believed was a growing gap between rich and poor.[22] This last theme became even more prominent in Pope Paul VI's 1968 encyclical *Populorum Progressio,* a document notable for its pronounced bias against capitalist forms of development.[23] As in the late nineteenth and early twentieth centuries, the Roman discussion of political economy in the mid-twentieth century gave little impetus to the development in American Catholicism of an ethic of wealth creation.

Such a development was further impeded by the influence in postconciliar American Catholicism of those Latin American theologies of liberation whose animus toward market-oriented economies made Paul VI look virtually Manchesterian by comparison.[24] The North American ground for the reception of liberation theology had already been prepared, in activist and intellectual circles, by the influence of the Catholic Worker movement, whose founders Peter Maurin and Dorothy Day emphasized, respectively, corporatist and anarchist approaches to issues of politics and economics— the common thread between these two rather divergent views being a profound distaste for capitalism.[25]

Missed Opportunities

If ideas have a social location—if, in other words, ideas require a favorable climate and soil in which to take root, grow, and develop—then it turns out that there was little reason to expect that American Catholicism would evolve a theology, ethics, and spirituality of entrepreneurship before World War II, and indeed before the 1960s. American Catholics, before that decade, were overwhelmingly working class; their economic concerns were with matters of wealth distribution, not wealth creation; and their formal religious leadership (while showing a healthy respect for capitalism's successes, particularly as these bore on the financial circumstances of the church) evinced little interest in helping develop such a theology, ethics, and spirituality.

Changed demographic circumstances, however, ought to have led to changed attitudes and ideas on this matter of an ethic of wealth creation. There can be no doubt that contemporary American Catholics live in different economic and social conditions from those of their parents and grandparents. American Catholicism is still, in many respects, an immigrant church; one-quarter of German-American and Irish-American Catholics, 52 percent of Polish-American Catholics, and 72 percent of Italian-American Catholics are either first generation (that is, foreign-born) or second generation. These sons and daughters of immigrants have done spectacularly well in the United States. American Catholics are second in family income to American Jews, and thus ahead of American Episcopalians, Presbyterians, Methodists, Lutherans, and Baptists. American Catholics, as a whole, are even with the national averages in educational attainment and occupational prestige; and the older immigrants, the German-American and Irish-American Catholics, are above the national average on these indices.[26] Given these data, the classic nativist canard that the Catholic tradition would create obstacles to Catholics' full participation in American economic, social, and political life seems more absurd than ever (its occasional reappearances on the editorial page of the *New York Times* notwithstanding). In fact, as suggested above, there may well be distinctively Catholic habits of mind and institutional circumstances that favored Catholic accomplishment in America.

This contemporary pattern of economic and social success—the rapid and dramatic transformation of American Catholicism in the postwar period from an urban, working-class church to a church of the suburban middle and upper middle classes—should have created the sociological conditions for the development of a theology, ethics, and spirituality of wealth creation. Indeed, some probes toward such a development have been made;[27] but they are just that, probes, and those who have made them are regarded with attitudes ranging from faint amusement to barely disguised contempt by the current American Catholic intellectual establishment.

Why has this happened? The answer again lies in the social location of ideas. Parallel to the rise of what we might call the Catholic CEO class over the past generation, there has developed a new class of Catholic intellectuals and publicists. These people are highly influential (through the prominent Catholic opinion journals, through seminaries and universities) and bureaucratically well positioned (at both the diocesan and national levels, and in religious communities), and they bear a standard "new class" animus toward the old business-class elite—which now just happens to be composed, in significant part, of the Catholic new class's coreligionists.[28]

Those who appreciate Peter Rossi's *mot* that there are many ironies in the fire will doubtless find confirmation for the ironic view of history in this situation. At the precise moment when the socioeconomic conditions in American Catholicism were ripe for the development of an ethic of wealth creation, the main intellectual and opinion switchboards in the American church were in the hands of a new class of intellectuals and activists whose attitudes toward capitalism were, at best, frosty. Others will find in this situation a confirmation of their judgment that capitalism's great weakness is its seeming inability to generate persuasive and evocative myths that legitimate its empirically undeniable material successes; and then the argument will proceed as to whether this is an "intrinsic incapacity" (*pace* Peter L. Berger) or the result of not enough people paying enough attention to the problem (*pace* Michael Novak). Be that as it may, the fact remains that the current sociological openness to the development of an ethic of wealth creation in American Catholicism is being actively impeded by the emergence of the Catholic new class, whose anticapitalist bias is scarcely less vehement than that of John Hughes or Orestes Brownson.[29]

The tension between the facts of American Catholic economic and social achievement on the one hand, and the ideological biases of the American Catholic new class on the other, was one dynamic in the generation, gestation, and production of the American bishops' 1986 national pastoral letter, "Economic Justice for All." The process leading to the writing of that letter was set in train by a motion at the 1980 annual meeting of the National Conference of Catholic Bishops. That meeting had adopted a (singularly ignored, if well-argued) "Pastoral Letter on Marxist Communism," and Hartford auxiliary bishop Peter Rosazza proposed that the bishops devote a pastoral letter to capitalism, in order to be "balanced."[30] Bishop Rosazza's motion was accepted, and the mandate of the drafting committee was expanded so that the pastoral letter to follow would address the full range of issues involved in American economic life.

Like the bishops' 1983 letter, "The Challenge of Peace," "Economic Justice for All" had a specific historic focus: the Reagan administration, and all its works, and all its array. Reagan administration rhetoric and policy on nuclear weapons and strategy had been influential (some would say determinative) in motivating the bishops to issue "The Challenge of Peace,"[31] and similar vectors of influence were doubtless at work in shaping "Economic Justice for All," which, viewed from one angle, is a principled and lengthy objection to the supply-side revolution.

This is not the place to analyze "Economic Justice for All" in detail. Suffice it to say that the pastoral letter did little to advance the development of an ethic of wealth creation in American Catholicism. The pastoral's biblical section, although it began with a brief reflection on divine creativity in the world, was primarily focused on the virtue of justice, which was understood largely in terms of distributive justice.[32] The pastoral's exhortations addressed "blue collar workers, managers, homemakers, politicians, and others,"[33] but not entrepreneurs. The bishops wrote that they wished to "encourage and support a renewed sense of vocation in the business community,"[34] but that vocation was never discussed in terms of the creation of wealth.

It may well be the case, as John Langan, S. J., has argued, that "Economic Justice for All" was "more accepting of the patterns of U.S. capitalism than are standard presentations of Catholic social thought as a middle ground or third way between capitalism and socialism."[35] The bishops' pastoral is not actively hostile to the development of an ethic and spirituality of entrepreneurship; but such a development is not among the various urgent items on the ecclesiastical agenda sketched by "Economic Justice for All." In this respect, at least, the 1986 pastoral letter represents an episcopal culmination of the pattern of American Catholic missed opportunities that has unfolded in recent years under the influence, not of a working-class constituency, but of a new-class intellectual elite hostile toward market-oriented economies and the business class.[36]

Elements of an American Catholic Ethic of Wealth Creation

Materials are not lacking for the development of a Catholic ethic of wealth creation with special resonance in the United States. Among the ample resources to be tapped are the following.

The creation-centered social thought of John Paul II. Catholic socialists acclaim John Paul II for leading an alleged opening to the Left.[37] This interpretation of the encyclicals *Laborem Exercens* and *Sollicitudo Rei Socialis* is shared (minus the acclaim, of course) by some Catholic conservatives.[38] Although it is true that the pope's personal preferences seem to lie in the direction of some sort of social democracy (an inclination he shares with many other northern and eastern European intellectuals), John Paul's most distinctive contribution to the development of modern Catholic social thought has been in a decidedly entrepreneurial direction, in his identification (in *Sollicitudo*) of a "right of economic initiative."[39]

The pope's definition of this right is located within that creation-centered theology of the person to which he devoted considerable attention in his inaugural encyclical, *Redemptor Hominis,* and which forms the foundation of the pope's theology of work in *Laborem Exercens.* In the latter, for example, the pope writes that "The word of God's revelation is profoundly marked by the fundamental truth that man, created in the image of God, shares by his work in the activity of the creator and that, within the limits of his own human capabilities, man in a sense continues to develop that activity, and perfects it as he advances further and further in the discovery of the resources and values contained in the whole of creation."[40]

In *Sollicitudo,* the pope takes the discussion an important step further and identifies "economic initiative" (or what others might term entrepreneurship or wealth creation) with "the creative subjectivity of the citizen"—a reflection in history and society of that divine creativity that began, and sustains, this world. Wealth creation, on this analysis, is a specifically economic form of human participation in God's abiding creativity, God's sustaining care for his creation.[41]

Writing prior to the publication of *Sollicitudo,* the Lay Commission on Catholic Social Teaching and the U.S. Economy suggested that the Roman magisterium had not paid adequate attention to entrepreneurship as an expression of human creativity "under God":

> Catholic social thought has not yet put sufficient emphasis upon the creative instrument through which new ideas and inventions are brought into service to human beings: the practical insight of the entrepreneur. By themselves, brilliant ideas do not serve humankind; to be brought into service to man, they must be transformed through complex processes of design and production. The talent to perform this transformation is as rare and humanly precious as talent in any other field. Indeed, the promotion of entrepreneurial talent is indispensable if the "cry of the poor" is to be heard. If not the man or woman of enterprise, who else will create new wealth? Who else will invent new opportunities for employment?[42]

It would be going too far to claim that *Sollicitudo Rei Socialis* clearly identifies entrepreneurship as the key to economic justice for all; but the pope's endorsement of the "right of economic initiative" does suggest that the Roman magisterium is more open to the moral case for democratic capitalism than it has ever been in the past—and that openness is the prerequisite to a moral legitimation of entrepreneurship. Moreover, the pope's location of this right within the framework of his creation-centered theology of the human person ought to be attractive to Americans, taught by Jefferson that "the God Who gave us life, gave us liberty, at the same time."

The "preferential option for the poor." The ubiquitous formulation, "the preferential option for the poor" (which Peter L. Berger once described as sounding like "a bad English translation of a bad Spanish translation of a bad German idea"), is generally taken to be the slogan of those who would look last, if at all, to capitalism, entrepreneurship, and economic initiative as the means to bring about economic justice for all. Conversely, the tendency of those of us who look precisely to the capitalist revolution for the effective pursuit of that morally desirable end is usually to abandon the phrase and even the concept of a "love of preference for the poor" (in Cardinal Joseph Ratzinger's reformulation). This is, I think, a mistake.

It is a mistake, first, because the "preferential option" language has become embedded in the contemporary Catholic discourse, even at the official level,[43] and no amount of kvetching seems likely to dislodge it in the foreseeable future. The "preferential option" or "love of preference" for the poor is here to stay. And matters of euphony notwithstanding, the real issue is the content that is put into the phrase.

Second, it is a mistake for the entrepreneurially oriented to assume that the preferential option must necessarily involve a state-centered or market-deprecating approach to economic life and social change. This, argues Dennis McCann, is not what the authors of "Economic Justice for All" had in mind when they endorsed the preferential option. The American bishops' letter, McCann suggests, treats the preferential option in formal terms as a "middle axiom" whose substantive content is primarily evangelical rather than political or economic. "The option for the poor is clearly meant to be imitative of Christ's way of acting," writes McCann; it does not call the church into class struggle, it does not confer a "hermeneutic privilege" (that is, a greater ability to discern the truth) on those whose incomes fall below a certain level, and it does not necessarily drive Catholic social thought away from market-oriented approaches to economic development and empowerment.[44] In their endorsement of the preferential option, the American bishops "are defining a moral litmus test for a just society that is both an authentic reflection of the religious vision animating Catholic social teaching and an appropriate expression of our common moral aspirations as Americans"[45]—nothing less than that, but nothing more, either.

McCann rightly notes that his interpretation of the bishops' use of the "preferential option" formulation will be disappointing to "partisans of liberation theology"; but it ought to be attractive to those who are convinced, first, that there is no way around the formulation in the contemporary Catholic debate and, second, that entrepreneurship, enterprise, and economic initiative—capitalism, in other words—are the instruments most likely to help the poor get out of poverty. If the preferential option is a middle axiom, whose function is to be understood formally, then the substantive debate remains wide open, and the question of precisely how to exercise the option can be argued on grounds favorable to those who would press the capitalist case, namely, the empirical grounds sketched by Peter L. Berger in *The Capitalist Revolution.*[46]

"Economic Justice for All"—and its guiding middle axiom, the "preferential option for the poor"—can thus, with a bit of hermeneutic judo, become an ally in the evolution of an American Catholic ethic of wealth creation.

The social analysis of Jacques Maritain. Ralph McInerny, rereading Jacques Maritain's *Reflections on America* some thirty years after its original publication, was struck by the Frenchman's thoughts about American capitalism. In his *Integral Humanism,* Maritain had taken a rather hostile attitude toward capitalism as a system "grounded on the principle of the fecundity of money and the absolute primacy of individual profit"; but, in America, that hotbed of capitalist enterprise, Maritain discovered a people who "were freedom-loving and mankind-loving . . . , people clinging to the importance of ethical standards, anxious to save the world, the most humane and the least materialist among modern peoples which had reached the industrial age."[47]

America was not a materialist nation; there was "no avarice in the American cast of mind." Americans frankly recognized that money was important, and this disturbed some Europeans; but, Maritain argued, "the ordinary course of American institutions and the innumerable American private groups show us that the ancient Greek and Roman idea of the *civis praeclarus,* the dedicated citizen who spends his money in the service of the common good, plays an essential part in the American consciousness." The notion of American materialism, Maritain concluded, was "no more than a curtain of silly gossip and slander."[48]

It is striking that "Economic Justice for All," a document whose footnotes include references to Richard Barnet, Gar Alperovitz, Michael Harrington, and E. F. Schumacher, did not find occasion to cite (or even refer its readers to) *Reflections on America.* Charity, and holding open the possibility of the hermeneutic judo suggested above, forbids speculation as to why. However, any ethic of wealth creation in American Catholicism is going to have to confront not only the drumbeat of new-class criticism about American greed but also Maritain's claim that American materialism is, at the very least, of a very distinctive sort. The development of such an ethic will require careful reflection on current patterns of philanthropy and private charitable giving in the United States, taking the good news (that personal and corporate giving has risen throughout the 1980s) along with the bad (that today's American Catholics, despite their economic advantages, are giving to their church in a far less generous manner than their parents or grandparents).

Other Things to Think About

An emerging American Catholic ethic of wealth creation should also address the following concerns.

Leisure. A classically grounded Catholic ethic of wealth creation will have to confront, and might well incorporate, the analysis of Josef Pieper in his *Leisure: The Basis of Culture.*[49] The simple-minded may regard Pieper's work as reflecting the kind of Catholic lassitude and lack of interest in the real world of commerce that was overcome by the northern European Protestant ethic during the Industrial Revolution. Pieper's book, however, does not so much argue against the work ethic as attempt to locate that ethic within a broader cultural horizon so that the question "Work for what?" gets due attention. Work, as John Paul II has insisted, is an expression of human creativity, and man works precisely in order to "elevate increasingly the cultural and moral level of the society in which he lives in community with those who belong to the same family."[50] Moreover, human beings exercise their divinely mandated creativity in a dialectic of work and leisure: "Man ought to imitate God both in working and also in resting, since God himself wished to present his own creative activity under the form of work and rest."[51] The world of work is not a more real world than the world of leisure; rather, work and leisure are two moments in the unfolding dialectic of human creativity under God.

This classic Catholic discussion may have a particular relevance for the contemporary American scene in view of the plethora of books and conferences urging the United States to be more like Japan because "Japan is number one." "More like Japan" usually means more ruthlessly meritocratic and hierarchical; more locked into the notion of work and wealth creation as ends in themselves, with little or no connection to the world of leisure; more, to use an otherwise troubling neologism from the modern Roman magisterium, "economistic." Perhaps those characteristics of modern Japanese society give Japan a comparative advantage in some aspects of international trade and finance; but it is not self-evident that America must, or indeed should, imitate them, since they would seem to involve cultural trade-offs that we may not wish to make. In any event, Pieper's analysis of leisure and culture, and John Paul II's dialectic of work and rest, ought to be incorporated into the discussion of an American Catholic ethic of wealth creation, on their own merits and as an antidote to that new form of works righteousness that marches under the banner of "Japan is number one."

Spirituality and vocation. An ethic of wealth creation will have to address the question of spirituality in a society of abundance. Chesterton's observation that "there is more simplicity in the man who eats caviar on impulse than in the man who eats grape-nuts on principle" may give little comfort to the health faddists among us (and that in itself is no small recommendation for GKC's insight); but it reminds us that interior disposition is at least as significant a dimension of the spiritual life as external practice—a Christian understanding with a long pedigree, dating back to the parable of the Pharisee and the publican (Luke 18:9–14).

Gilbert Meilaender has identified three dispositions, each with an honorable history in Christian thought, toward possessions:

1. Possessions are both a dangerous threat and a good opportunity. To avoid the dangers, we need the virtue of *simplicity*—to choke off the passion for things and moderate our desires. To seize the opportunities for service, we need the virtue of *generosity.*

2. Regularly seizing the opportunity to give to those in need may call for and give rise to something more than a moderation of our desires; it may suggest the need for *renunciation.* Clement [of Alexandria] writes to oppose this move, and he is surely correct to see that not all Christians are called to such a life—correct also to see that this is no higher life, since it can offer no guarantee of a purer inner spirit. What Jesus says to the rich ruler is the precise truth: *no one* is good but God alone. . . .

3. An attempt to practice the virtues of simplicity and generosity may give rise to a sense of *tension* within the Christian life—tension that pushes the whole of that life in a relatively *austere* direction. Presupposing the possession of goods, the virtue of generosity seems . . . to call simply for a right inner spirit and by itself sets no limit (other than the neighbor's need) to what we possess. Presupposing the danger of possessions, the virtue of simplicity reminds us that things are not simply neutral. Too much—though also too little—can corrupt the soul.[52]

There is no simple answer to the related questions of interior disposition and public practice in this matter of wealth, its uses, and its temptations. But Meilaender's reflections on what we might call the "tug toward austerity" in classic Christian spirituality should not be taken as antipathetic toward an ethic of wealth creation, particularly if that ethic is lived out in a vocationally serious effort to serve others. Wealth creation need not, in other words, result in its creators becoming self-aggrandizing wastrels. Not all entrepreneurs are Donald Trump, and no serious Christian entrepreneur will find his vocational compass oriented toward conspicuous consumption.

Meilaender also reminds us that austerity is not a good in itself. We can, writes Meilaender, "retreat from the life of society; we may choose subsistence for ourselves";[53] but to do that is also to retreat "from a life of exchange and interdependence into a life of autonomy and independence."[54] Such a retreat is no guarantee of virtue, and is quite possibly as much a threat to virtue as the temptations of overconsumption.

The key to public Christian life within the tension Meilaender identifies—the tension between the parable of the talents and Jesus' saying about camels and needles—may well lie in one's willingness to live a vocational, as distinguished from a careerist, life. Not all Christians, not all Catholics, are called to be entrepreneurs and creators of wealth; but some surely are, and in living that vocation as a matter of service to others, the entrepreneur is participating in that godly creativity which is man's distinguishing characteristic. Some Christians are, conversely, called to a life of service to others and austerity, even radical austerity; but that call is not, by itself, a ticket to spiritual eminence. For some it may well be; for others it can lead to the worst forms of pride and hubris.

Meilaender's summary statement is an important one for those interested in developing an ethic of wealth creation, and ought to be pondered as well by those who regard such a project as inherently inferior in vocational terms:

> Room must be left for freedom of the Christian life—and, perhaps still more, freedom of the God who calls Christians to different ways of life. Beneficence to others in need is a duty for all Christians, but the ways in which that beneficence may be enacted are many, and no single way can be universally required.[55]

Conclusion

I will conclude by returning to the questions posed at the beginning of this chapter.

There is nothing in the theological core of Roman Catholic social thought that precludes the development of an ethic of wealth creation, and much that might in fact point toward it. Contemporary Catholic theology's emphasis on the analogy between divine and human creativity (as developed by the Karol Wojtyla, not the Matthew Fox, wing of the church!) is one important theological foundation for the development of such an ethic. The classic Catholic social and ethical principle of subsidiarity, which, inter alia, seeks to set boundaries to the pretensions of the modern state, would also seem to favor entrepreneurial and market-oriented approaches to economics, rather than state-centered or central-planning models. So, too, would the parallel social-ethical principle of personalism, particularly when it emphasizes the virtue of creativity. In *Sollicitudo Rei Socialis,* we may indeed see the beginnings of a move toward the moral legitimation, indeed celebration, of some forms of entrepreneurship on the part of the Roman magisterium.

On the other hand, it should be frankly admitted that such a move will involve a kind of development of social doctrine, for there is much in the economic and political analysis of the classics of modern Catholic social thought—and particularly in *Quadragesimo Anno* and *Populorum Progressio*—that points in a rather different direction. Whether that is the result of an anticapitalist bias per se, or whether it reflects more generalized Roman concerns about modernization, is a question worth further exploration. That exploration will be complicated by the fact that there is a concerted effort under way today, by publicists such as Gregory Baum in Canada and Dale Vree in the United States, to claim John Paul II's social teaching for the democratic socialist camp. That effort, however implausible it may appear, will reinforce the problems for an evolving ethic of wealth creation posed by the generally anticapitalist animus of the American Catholic new class.

Still, there is more readiness for such an evolution in contemporary American Catholicism than there has been at any time in our history. The immigrant church of the working class has been transformed into the suburban church of the middle and upper middle class. That transformation is not without its own difficulties and tensions; but it also creates the sociological conditions for the possibility of an ethic of wealth creation in American Catholicism. Whether that opportunity will be seized—for the benefit of the poor, as well as for the moral legitimation of the entrepreneurs—is, of course, another question.

Private Property, Ethics, and Wealth Creation

I t is important to develop an ethic of wealth creation. For all too long, excessive attention has been paid to the morality of wealth distribution. But economic creation is logically prior to distribution; unless the first is accomplished, the second becomes irrelevant.[1] If we are to preserve and even expand the capitalist order, the only system that has been successful in creating wealth on a vast scale and over many decades, we shall have to mobilize all the resources at our command. A sound economic understanding, although necessary for the attainment of this noble goal, is hardly sufficient. The capitalist system cannot long endure if it concedes the moral high ground to its detractors. We must harness the heart as well as the head.

Fortunately, there is a philosophy ideally suited to our task: libertarianism.[2] This philosophy provides the ethical perspective necessary for economic efficiency and for the enhancement of wealth production. I shall begin by setting out the basic premises of this philosophy, and shall then apply them to issues such as socialism, capitalism, economic regulation, and the welfare state.

I shall conclude with a discussion of the compatibility of libertarianism and religious belief.

Libertarianism

The basic premise of libertarianism is that, at least toward one another, we are all self-owners.[3] That is to say, and it is to say no more than this, that it is improper for anyone else to invade our bodies, whether through enslavement, murder, rape, the military draft,[4] assault and battery, or any other act. An implication of this moral axiom is that it is illegitimate to initiate coercion against a person who does not first himself undertake a physically abusive act. This is the nonaggression axiom, a defining characteristic of libertarianism, or voluntarism.[5] One may defend oneself against attack, or even retaliate—libertarianism is not equated with pacifism—but one may not be the first to assault another. Libertarianism is a political philosophy and a philosophy of law, not a philosophy of life. It asks one solitary question—under what conditions is the use of physical force justified?—and gives one solitary answer: only when a prior use of physical force was engaged in.

What are the alternatives to self-ownership? One possibility is some variant of autocracy, monarchy, or totalitarianism, where one person, or a small group of people, possesses the right to dispose of the lives of all others. This, however, is in stark violation of the moral requirement of generalizability or universalizability. What is so ethically special about this person or small group that makes them deserve to rule everyone else? Since there is no such distinguishing moral characteristic in existence,[6] this scenario falls to the ground.

The only other option besides self-ownership is that we all own a 1/nth share of everyone on earth, where n equals the total population. In this vision, or rather nightmare, no one would be allowed to so much as scratch himself, without obtaining permission from the rightful owners of his body, that is, everyone else. If direct democracy were practiced under these conditions, the human race would quickly die out (relieving us of the problem of solving this dilemma), since it would be too cumbersome to get everyone else's permission to do anything. If indirect, that is, representative, democracy were observed, the situation would soon deteriorate into an autocratic scenario—which has already been rejected.

One can justify self-ownership on the further ground that its denial amounts to a "performative contradiction";[7] one could not even utter the claim that no person's body belongs to himself without using some body parts (such as the vocal cords and lungs). To use one's body in this way would, however, be to contradict, and thus undercut, the claim.

A second premise of libertarianism is that a person's legitimately held private property shall likewise be safe from invasion.[8] All that is meant by private property rights is that human beings can utilize physical items of the earth without necessarily committing an invasive act.[9] If people do not have such rights, and yet insist upon acting noninvasively, we must all perish; for we cannot live without using earth, air, water, fire, and all the things we can create out of them. If we are to survive under such a flawed understanding of property, then we must all act intrusively: we must use that which according to the theory we have no right to use.

The real question is not whether human beings have property rights; it is, rather: How shall they be divided up? May they be individual, or must they be communal? These are the questions to which I now turn.

Private Property Rights

We can justify private property rights along lines similar to those we used for justifying individual self-ownership of our bodies, and for rejecting communal ownership of them. Again, there exist three options: individual ownership of property, group ownership of everything in common, and autocratic control. Autocratic control is not universalizable; and if each of the six billion of us had to get the permission of the other 5,999,999,999 before anyone could begin to use the resources of the earth, we would all starve—or be forced to submit to a system of autocratic rule. Utilizing the nonaggression axiom, we may say that any means of obtaining property that is strictly voluntary is justified.[10] Some examples are trade, gifts, gambling, inheritance, charity, investments, employment, borrowing, and repayment of debts. If A has legitimate title to property y, and trades it for B's legitimately held z, then A becomes the new and proper owner of z, and likewise B of y.

How do unowned parts of nature pass into ownership by humans? The answer to this question is less fully settled than those elements of the libertarian philosophy already introduced; the answer is, through homesteading. In the words of Locke one "mixes one's labor with the land" and thereby obtains rightful title.[11] One way to justify this procedure is again to contrast it with its alternatives. In what other ways can property pass from a state of nature into human ownership? There seem to be but three alternatives: claims, government sales, and communal ownership. Under the first alternative, we can establish rightful title to land merely by claiming it. The difficulty with this is that many people may claim the same property, leaving the ownership in dispute. Moreover, this seems unsatisfactory to our moral sense. The claimers did nothing to earn this property; why should they be able to own it, and thus prevent others from using it? The second alternative has the drawback that governments are only composed of flesh-and-blood people, none of whom can justify their claim to unowned land. What is so special about the bureaucrat that she should be entitled to possess unowned land, merely because she is a part of the government?[12] As for the third alternative, the case for it dissolves when we realize that in practice it would mean either that such a resource could not be used (the costs of getting billions of people to agree on its use would be catastrophic) or that all such resources would end up, in effect, being owned by a few rulers.[13]

Socialism or Capitalism?

It is of the utmost importance to realize that libertarianism by no means implies a capitalist form of organization. The view that the recognition of private property rights logically implies a capitalist mode must be adamantly rejected. Libertarianism is every bit as compatible with socialism as it is with capitalism.[14] How is this possible? Let us clarify this point with the following diagram:

	Socialism	Capitalism
Voluntarism	voluntary socialism	laissez-faire capitalism
Coercivism	coercive socialism	state capitalism

Although most political economic theorists identify socialism and capitalism as polar opposites, and play off the one against the other, I shall completely reject this mode of analysis. The relevant distinction is not between socialism and capitalism, but between voluntarism and coercivism. The major combatants on the field thus are not socialism versus capitalism, but rather voluntary socialism and voluntary capitalism on the one side, arrayed against the forces of coercive socialism and coercive capitalism, in unholy alliance, on the other.

Before considering the four boxes in the diagram, let us begin by describing the rows, and then the columns. I have already touched upon the distinction between voluntarism and coercivism. Voluntarism is the condition wherein the libertarian axiom of nonaggression against nonaggressors is respected and upheld; coercivism is the situation where that axiom is violated. A strictly voluntary system is clearly compatible with libertarianism—indeed, the two are equated—whereas coercion is the diametric opposite of this philosophy.

Now for the columns. I understand socialism to mean adherence to the familiar Marxist doctrine "from each according to his abilities, to each according to his needs," as well as to the view that all property (or at least all capital goods) shall be held in common. The crucial question for libertarianism is whether these socialistic concepts are put into effect on a voluntary or on a coercive basis. We are all familiar with coercive or state socialism (communism), where the socialistic doctrines are upheld, at least in theory,[15] but this is done coercively. Individuals have no right to opt out of the system, nor is their consent necessary in order to begin it or to justify its continued existence.

In sharp contradistinction to coercive socialism is its polar opposite, voluntary socialism. Examples include the kibbutz, the cooperative, the commune, the labor union run on voluntaristic principles, the Hutterite colony, and the monastery. The typical nuclear family, moreover, is a voluntary socialist commune![16] All members of the family consume not in accordance with their ability to earn, but based on their needs. The parents may earn the entire income, but certainly do not consume it all; young children earn none of it, but consume on the basis of their needs. In all these cases, voluntarism is strictly upheld.[17] No one is dragged, kicking and screaming, into voluntary socialism, nor prevented from leaving. Nor does the voluntary commune seize the private property of those who have not joined it of their own free will. On the contrary, the property of the commune is a pooling of the legitimately owned resources of the individuals who constitute it. This form of socialism fully lives up to the requirements of voluntarism; hence, it is entirely compatible with libertarianism.[18]

I understand capitalism to mean a system of interactions based on trade, employment, interest rates, business firms, profits, and so on. An aphorism parallel to the socialist one quoted earlier might be: "From each according to his abilities, to each according to his abilities." Just as for socialism, there is a bifurcation in capitalism. Under the laissez-faire or voluntary variety, the businessperson earns his or her profits only from the consensual purchases of the consumers; "consumer sovereignty" is the catchphrase of the free enterprise system.[19] Whenever a trade takes place—whether a trade of one good for another (barter), of a good or service for money (sale), or of money for labor services (employment)—both parties gain, at least in their own *ex ante* expectations, compared to the situation that obtained before the trade took place and that would have continued in the absence of the trade.

If I trade you one hour of my time for a salary of $5, this must mean that I consider that hour to be worth less to me than the $5; and it must mean that you value the services you expect to obtain from me more highly than that amount of money. Thus, we both gain in welfare from the trade.[20] The free market consists of the totality of all such voluntary trades that take place in a given area. We are thus in a position to claim that the market benefits all participants![21]

Not all versions of capitalism are quite so benign, however. The system of state capitalism (or monopoly capitalism, or economic fascism, or corporate capitalism—or, paradoxically, national socialism, that is, Nazism) retains a thin veneer of adherence to free enterprise institutions. But this is only a mask of the underlying reality. In fact, the corporate interests seize, through government, that which would be unavailable to them through the market. If the customers purchase a given product in sufficient quantity and at a high enough price to allow the ruling class the profit it deems adequate, well and good. Free markets may well be allowed to obtain for that one small sector. If not, however, then through a series of protections, payoffs, taxes, subsidies, bailouts, franchises, permits, licenses, quotas, bribes, exemptions, and tariffs the rulers will expropriate these funds from the general public.

Consider the typical business bailout, for instance. The corporation confiscates, through taxes from the citizenry, those funds that were not forthcoming to them in the form of voluntary purchases. In effect, the corporation does an end run around the consumer. It asks its agent, the government, to appropriate monies from all members of society, in the form of taxes, and then to turn this wealth over to the corporate interests in the form of a bailout.[22]

This distinction between laissez-faire capitalism and state monopoly capitalism (the two boxes in the right-hand column of the diagram) is subtle and difficult to understand. It is even harder to perceive than the distinction between voluntary and coercive socialism (the two boxes in the left-hand column of the diagram). Nevertheless, it is one of the most fundamental of all distinctions in political economy. Its importance would be hard to overestimate. So let me reiterate. There is a world of difference between defending a system of competition, the free marketplace, in which all businesses must sink or swim depending upon how well they satisfy consumers, and defending particular business enterprises (for example, by giving them a monopoly franchise or a protective tariff). The latter, indeed, can fairly be characterized as a "running dog" policy in behalf of capitalist interests; but not the former, the libertarian vision. If that vision is the running dog of anything, it is of the consumer; if it speaks in behalf of anything, it is of liberty, justice, and individual rights, not special business interest groups.

In the felicitous phrase of Nozick, laissez-faire permits all "capitalist acts between consenting adults."[23] For the philosophy of libertarianism, however, a system that allows all socialist acts between consenting adults is equally legitimate. It is not the capitalism or the socialism that is important;[24] the debate between capitalism and socialism has been for too long a red herring that has been allowed to obfuscate serious political and economic analysis. It is the amount of coercion or voluntarism in a system that really matters.

The Welfare State

Now that we have set the stage with an introduction to libertarianism, we are ready to consider its applications to that public policy issue which perhaps more than any other strikes to the root of the ethic of wealth creation: the welfare system.

It is a challenging task to show that the welfare state fails the test of economic efficiency; that it is inconsistent not only with the libertarian ethic of wealth creation, but with morality in general. One reason for the difficulty of this task is that numerous high-profile advocates of capitalism have actually made their peace with the welfare state and now defend it from attack, instead of indicating how and why it is incompatible with ethical considerations.[25]

In the libertarian perspective, the ideal situation would be one where there was no welfare state at all. This institution is demeaning to recipients; it creates dependency; and it reduces self-reliance.[26] A large part of the need for the welfare state is created by the excessive influence of government itself.[27] Minimum wage laws and collective bargaining legislation create poverty by increasing unemployment, especially for teenagers and unskilled workers. Rent control promotes homelessness by reducing the incentive to supply low-rental housing. Tariffs, quotas, and other international barriers to trade all make consumer purchases more expensive.[28] These examples are only the tip of the iceberg;[29] some other unwise government interferences with the market, which create poverty, are: usury laws; taxi medallions; marketing boards; regional development policies; public-sector ownership; plant-closing legislation; land zoning; price supports; government unemployment insurance; antitrust legislation; prohibition of such activities as speculating, insider trading, and other white-collar, victimless crimes; and barriers to entry such as immigration restrictions, medical licenses, permits, safety standards, and building codes.[30] These, too, boomerang, and achieve results that are the very opposite of those hoped for by their proponents.[31]

It is also obvious that these initiatives are inconsistent with the ethic of private property and individual ownership. The rights of at least one person are always violated; innocent people are forced to undertake acts they would not otherwise do (seek permits, licenses, or franchises in order to take part in commercial life), or are prevented from engaging in activities they would otherwise take part in (such as buying, selling, working, or immigrating). More often, it is the rights of both parties to engage in a voluntary capitalist act (a trade at mutually negotiated prices) that are abridged.

In all of these cases, and there are many more, government creates or exacerbates poverty. Some people of good will then expect government to alleviate the poverty that its own policies have created. Surely it is more sensible to ask government to stop creating the poverty in the first place; then we would have little or no need for its welfare-system solution.

However, even if government were not busily creating poverty, there would still be unfortunate people such as the mentally handicapped, the halt, the lame, the blind, the sick, quadriplegics, and mothers with infant children. A caring, compassionate society would still need some sort of welfare system.

Given that some sort of welfare is necessary, private-sector solutions, such as charity, are vastly preferably to the government variety.[32] When people give to charity, they do so on a voluntary basis. Nobody forces anyone at the point of a gun to contribute. When we do this through the compulsory tax system, the individual is told in effect that if he doesn't pay his taxes he will go to jail. This, to say the least, is coercive, and thus morally suspect.[33]

Moreover, private charity tends to be more responsive to the desires of the donors. If people determine that charity x is misusing their money, they can, on the basis of their own determination alone, divert resources to charity y. This, needless to say, cannot be accomplished when welfare is a government function.[34]

Further, almost all of the money in the private system actually goes to the poor. The Salvation Army estimates that between 93 and 97 percent of the money that it collects goes for its intended purpose.[35] The remainder is used for administrative purposes, such as the cost of collecting and disbursing the money. This is a record that many people in the public sector would find hard to meet. Sowell estimates that if the government's entire social welfare budget were just given to the poor instead of being administered by the government, the average poor family would have some $70,000 a year.[36] The fact that they don't have it shows that there are great leakages when the welfare function is not privatized.[37]

This leads us to the question of whether or not public welfare programs are really designed to help the poor. An attractive, though unpopular, hypothesis is that the people who benefit from such programs, and who are thus hurt by their elimination, are not the poor; rather, they are white-collar, highly educated, articulate members of the new class, many of them Marxist or leftist intellectuals. According to Lee:

> The poor are in the minority, are less likely to vote than more affluent citizens and are seldom organized into politically focussed groups. It is unlikely then that the poor will be very effective in the competition for political influence. Indeed, if the poor had the skills and attributes that are necessary for effective political action, they would not be poor. So while the political demands of the poor will no doubt push in the direction of increasing the funding for poverty programs, the magnitude of this influence will probably be small.

A more effectively organized and politically potent group with a vested interest in expanding government programmes to aid the disadvantaged is made up of those whose employment depends upon these programmes. These people include the several million people who are employed either directly by government welfare agencies or who, as private contractors and academic researchers, assist and advise these agencies. With the job security and income of these people tied to the funding of poverty, and poverty-related, programmes, they have a common and dominant interest in the continuation and expansion of this funding. When this focussed interest is coupled with the relative ease with which people can organize for political action through their employee organizations, poverty professionals become much more effective at obtaining political funding for poverty programmes than the poor themselves.[38]

In our mixed economy, it is the richer and better organized— including the "corporate welfare bums"—who get the lion's share of the welfare funding. Millions of dollars are spent for bailouts of rich corporations, which benefit their relatively wealthy stockholders. Highly organized artists and musicians, likewise, receive prince's ransoms, while literally pennies go for the really poor. Anyone who favors the poor, and the underdog, should be very suspicious of this public-sector means of channeling money to them, if for no other reason than that these means do not succeed.[39] All too often, the money is diverted to people who are far from poor.

Private charity, or private welfare, is much more efficient than the state counterpart.[40] The emphasis is on getting people back on their feet, not on instilling multigenerational dependency as is done in some advanced welfare states.[41] Traditionally, private charity was a task of the churches and other civic-minded organizations. Churches such as the Mormons, the Hutterites, the Catholics, the Dutch Church, and other Christian and non-Christian denominations have established estimable records of helping the poor; yet, paradoxically, some of the strongest objections to privatizing welfare now come from this quarter.

Let us suppose that needs remain unmet even under free enterprise and in the absence of a government causing poverty on a mass scale; so that even with an unstinting church and private effort there are still needs that are not met. In that case, I would introduce a second principle of welfare.

That principle is that if state welfare is necessary, it should be parsimonious, not generous to a fault as at present. Welfare of whatever kind should be as low as possible. Specifically, it should not be competitive with low-wage employment; otherwise, incentives decrease and family breakup ensues.

Perhaps the most notable example of the deleterious effects of welfarism run amok is the state of the black family in the United States. Tucker states:

> The facts about the black family are brutal. More than half the black children born in the U.S. today are illegitimate. Almost half of these, 23 percent of all black children, are born to unwed teenage mothers. Every year more black girls drop out of high school to have a baby than graduate from college. Over 50 percent of all black children are now bring raised in single parent households, meaning by unmarried black women. About 75 percent of all poor black children are in these families. This is a social tragedy of truly frightening proportions. It has never happened before in history. Mao Tse Tung's deliberate efforts to break up the nuclear family on the Chinese-ruled communes didn't have even a fraction of the effect that contemporary American social policies have had on black Americans.
>
> The welfare system makes an irresistible offer to every eligible female over the age of 16. It says to every black female teenager, you may be poor, you may have family problems and you may be discouraged about your future, but if you have a baby, right now, we will give you your own apartment, free medical care, food stamps and a regular income over the next 20 years. If you have another baby soon after, we will increase your allotment. How many black men, poor or even affluent, can match this offer? How many teenage girls anywhere, black or white, poor or affluent, can afford their own apartment at age 16? These teenage girls who dropped out of school and have babies are not ignorant. They are not morally weak. They are not sexually lascivious. They are simply rational human beings making the most intelligent choice on how to improve their economic condition.

Black families are not really breaking up at all. Instead, black families are no longer forming. When women start families, they no longer look for a husband, they simply marry the state.

Some commentators attempt to deny the view that black families have been savaged by government welfarism run amok by charging that blacks never had much of a family structure anyway. That is false. The black family was more than strong enough to survive the ordeal of slavery. There were cases of black men and women walking up and down the countryside after the Civil War searching for wives, husbands or children from whom they had become separated during the chaos and the conflict. Advertisements for lost spouses and children were still appearing in the black newspapers as late as the 1880s, 25 years after the Civil War.

This survival continued right through the 1930s. One study of ethnic groups in Boston in the early part of the century revealed that the rate of broken families among blacks was actually lower than among most other ethnic groups. Only around ten percent at a time when illegitimacy in Irish families was running over 30 percent.

Black social patterns were ruined only when liberals arrived on the scene in the 1930s with their aid to families with dependent children and other blandishments to let the state do for people what they aren't capable of doing for themselves. The tragedy occurred because blacks trusted the system. They didn't have the inherent suspicions to resist government assistance and avoid sympathetic bureaucrats like the plague as many ethnic groups did then and still do today. No, the black family was more than strong enough to survive slavery. It was just not strong enough to survive the welfare system.[42]

Let us now consider a sophisticated economic argument in favor of welfare programs, offered, paradoxically, by Milton Friedman:

It can be argued that private charity is insufficient because the benefits from it accrue to people other than those who make the gifts, a neighborhood effect. I am distressed by the sight of poverty; I am benefited by its alleviation; but I am benefited equally whether I or someone else pays for its alleviation; the benefits of other people's charity therefore partly accrue to me. To put it differently, we might all of us be willing to contribute to the relief of poverty *provided* everyone else did. We might not be willing to contribute the same amount without such assurance. In small communities, public pressure can suffice to realize the proviso even with private charity. In the large impersonal communities that are increasingly coming to dominate our society, it is much more difficult for it to do so.[43]

This is the oft-repeated argument of externalities, public goods, or neighborhood effects, also known as the free rider argument. One difficulty with this argument is that it proves too much. It could be used to justify any government expenditure—for the arts, rodeos, soap, lighthouses—provided only that it could be plausibly maintained that at least one person benefits from these activities over and above his or her payments for them.

Even if it were economically coherent, this argument is in direct violation of the libertarian ethic of noninvasion. It attempts to justify coercing people to do what they might otherwise choose not to do, namely, contribute their hard-earned money to the poor, even though they themselves are entirely innocent of any rights violations. However superficially appealing the argument, it is still invasive to forcibly alienate a person's property. In any other context, we would have no difficulty in identifying such an act as theft. Moreover, this externalities argument contradicts the axiom of positive economics that, as a science, economics is required to be neutral with respect to values. The economist's task is limited to explaining and understanding reality; the externalities argument, however, invites the economist to step out of his or her arena of expertise and take on a normative role.

It is, in fact, not at all clear that doing so will promote economic efficiency. Suppose, for example, that not all people share Friedman's tastes; suppose, that is, that the well-being of some is decreased by the prospect of other people receiving money in this manner. After all, not all people are alike—one man's meat is often another man's poison. Then, according to the logic of this argument, the state ought to prohibit all welfare, even private charity.

Epstein's argument is devastating:

> But who determines whether the probable external effects of welfare payments are positive or negative for unwilling contributors? Suppose X thinks that welfare payments are a dreadful mistake because they encourage individuals to survive on handouts instead of fending for themselves. He refuses to support all charitable activities, of any kind or description. If X obtains a political majority, should he be allowed in the name of the police power to ban charitable giving by others? If he cannot, then why can the majority exact his contributions from him? The refusal of any single individual to provide welfare payments does not prevent others from going ahead with their plans. Indeed, virtually all educational, religious, medical and welfare charities have long operated with the cooperation and financial support of only a tiny fraction of the total population.[44]

Foreign Aid

Let us now discuss the internationalization of the welfare state. Programs of this sort are usually referred to as "foreign aid," but this is a loaded term, in that it assumes that some sort of benefit for the masses of people is actually being created. A more neutral terminology would be "government-to-government transfers of funds."[45]

Unfortunately, the usual effect of such expenditures, benevolent intentions aside, is to prop up dictators by undergirding their centrally planned Marxist economic systems.[46] In the Soviet Union, for example, the 97 percent of the land that is farmed in the public sector accounts for only 75 percent of the crops. Private farming is allowed on only 3 percent of the land, but it accounts for fully 25 percent of the crops. There is famine in Ethiopia because of the Marxist dictatorship's imposition of price and other controls on agriculture, not because of drought or any other natural phenomenon.

The best way to remember the effects of international welfarism is to think of the three M's: Mercedeses, monuments, and machine guns. That is what the money really goes for. The starving children in the heartrending newspaper ads do not get this money. It is given to both Marxist and right-wing dictatorships, the ones who have run their economies into the ground.

These funds also exacerbate conflict in the recipient nations.[47] Foreign aid might only be 1 or 2 percent of the donor country's gross national product, but this is a significant amount of money in the third world. It is a much larger proportion of the receiving country's GNP. Many of these countries are organized along tribal lines; if the state were limited to the night-watchman role advocated by Adam Smith, it would not matter much who formed the government. But when the government is the be-all and end-all, making all sorts of life and death decisions, when government has vast amounts of foreign aid to distribute, then who is in control becomes crucially important. Competition for such control can lead to tribal warfare. In effect, tens of thousands of people have been killed because of well-intentioned foreign aid.

Welfare "Rights"

I shall now consider the welfare "rights" movement—a perversion of language if ever there was one, as can be seen by contrasting the negative rights of libertarianism or classical liberalism with the new-class idea of positive rights. Traditionally, negative rights were derived from the right to be free of violence. This right was entirely consistent with a philosophy of private property rights and with the nonaggression axiom. In the negative-rights view, all acts that do not invade anyone else's person or property may be engaged in; government is limited to providing police, an army, courts, fire protection . . . and, in some versions of the doctrine, a safety net under income, but only as a last resort. In contrast, there are the positive rights: the right to food, clothing, shelter, meaningful experiences. These are communal "rights," for the enforcement of which a coercive socialist state is needed.

Rights, no matter whether they are of the positive or negative sort, operate in such a way that if I have a right, you have an obligation. If I have a right to be left alone, you have an obligation to refrain from interfering with me or my property. If I have a right to food, you have an obligation to feed me. If I have a right to clothing, shelter, day care, you have an obligation to provide them for me.

Several points of contrast show the classical liberal concept of negative rights is tenable, whereas that of positive rights is not.

The first point concerns time. Negative rights are timeless. A million years ago the caveman had a right to be left alone. A hundred million years from now the spaceman will have an equal right not to be raped, murdered, or pillaged. We nowadays have a right to go unmolested as we walk down the street. The same does not hold for positive rights. Did the caveman have a right to a modern level of food, clothing, shelter, and medical care? This is absurd. A caveman had no right to running water or electricity, if for no other reason than it was impossible in those days to give them to him.

The second point concerns realism versus utopianism. We could, if we all resolved to, keep our mitts to ourselves and not murder, rape, or commit mayhem on other people. We could do this right now, if we all suddenly became so disposed. If we did, we would immediately have a world with no violations of negative rights. But could we, merely by resolving to, achieve a world where all positive-rights obligations are being met? No. It is simply impossible at this moment to give everyone in the world, all the people in India, Ethiopia, and China, the same level of income that North Americans now enjoy. This would require vastly more resources than are now available; it would take decades, even with the best will in the world, and with the full implementation of free markets, to accomplish this goal.

The third point has to do with human agency. Consider shipwrecks, droughts, typhoons. Do these phenomena involve negative-rights violations? No. Nobody's negative rights are violated because a human agent is needed in order for a violation to occur. There is no person responsible in these cases; they are acts of nature. But people's positive rights are violated, and on a massive scale, by hurricanes, for example. Houses are smashed to smithereens, people are killed outright, they have no food, no shelter, no clothing. The ludicrous result implied by the doctrine of positive rights is that acts of nature can violate rights.

The fourth point concerns game theory. If I have more positive rights, you have less of them. If I have more food, you have less food. It does not work that way with negative rights. If I have more peace and tranquility that does not necessarily mean that you have less. It is true that if I have more police protection, other things being equal, you have less. Police protection, however, requires goods and services; it is a positive right, not a negative one.

The fifth point concerns charity. In a regime of negative rights it is logically possible for charity to exist. If I give some money to a poor person, that is properly called charity. If there are positive rights, however, it is logically impossible for me to engage in a charitable act. If I attempt to do so, by offering someone some money, he or she could reply, "What do you mean by offering me charity? How dare you? That's not charity. I have a right to it. You are morally obliged to give it to me. I'm collecting this money as a debt."

If the philosophy of positive rights were consistently carried through, it would not merely be more difficult to practice charity, it would be logically impossible to do so. We would have eliminated in one fell swoop a perfectly good word from the English language. The very existence of the word "charity" is incompatible with the doctrine of positive rights. From this it may be deduced that since charity is indeed a meaningful word, the doctrine of positive rights is incorrect.

The sixth point has to do with Occam's razor. Simplicity is revered in science. We already have a phrase depicting the desiderata of the advocates of positive rights. What they are talking about is wealth. Why create a synonym for this perfectly good word in the English language? The only reason people concoct the etymological monstrosity "positive rights" is because we all subscribe to the view that if it is a right it has to be equal. We all have an equal right not to be molested, for example. The not-so-hidden agenda of the new-class intellectuals and other supporters of the welfare state is to perpetrate egalitarianism upon our society; and how better to do that than by tying their doctrines to the coattails of something we all respect, namely rights? These people ought to have the courage of their convictions; they ought to come out and call for greater equalization of wealth, if that is what they want, and not attempt to hide behind the doctrine of positive rights.

A lot of hypocrisy goes on with regard to the philosophy of equality. Its typical advocates own late-model automobiles, usually Volvos. They live in homes that would be the envy of people around the world, stuffed with furniture and knickknacks. They have expensive wristwatches and clothing. They have color televisions, video-cassette recorders, home computers, compact-disk music systems, and all sorts of fripperies and frivolities. And they piously utter platitudes about helping the poor. How do they reconcile their views with their opulent standards of living? If they seriously believe in their own professed ideology, why do they retain all this personal wealth? Why do they not give it away to the poor?

Another form of hypocrisy is distinguishing between North Americans and people in India or Afghanistan or Ethiopia. Why is it that citizens of the United States are more deserving of welfare than any other persons? If we are talking about human rights, surely the Bangladeshi is just as much human as is the American or Canadian. A welfare system that would make the North American recipient a very rich person indeed were he to live in Bangladesh can hardly be justified, especially on the egalitarian grounds of the welfare rights philosophy.

Here is another, related hypocrisy. Why just redistribute wealth? Why just money? Suppose we had a machine that could transfer beauty or IQ points or musical talent. Is it fair that Mozart exceeded me in musical talent, Einstein in intelligence, and Tom Selleck in beauty? Certainly not! Suppose there were a machine that could transfer IQ or beauty or talent from one person to another. Should we force those who have more of these attributes to share them, via this machine, with those of us who have less? That would be real equality, compared to which the cry for transfers of money from rich to poor pales into insignificance. Such a nightmare vision of positive rights is of course not compatible with negative liberty. Rather, it is part and parcel of a brave new world of indistinguishable, interchangeable human beings. That is where the philosophy of forced egalitarianism leads us to, ultimately.

What, if any, social services should the public sector ideally provide? The contention of libertarianism is: none. In the classical liberal tradition, government is used for defense, the judiciary, and police—not to take money away from Peter to give it to Paul. Such redistribution retards the incentives of both to increase their wealth through productive activity; and it is immoral to boot.

Religion and Libertarianism

What is the relationship between religion and libertarianism? At first glance there would appear to be little or no relationship, as a disproportionately high share of libertarians are irreligious.[48] This finding is buttressed by the fact that Ayn Rand, a militant and outspoken atheist, is the person who has had the greatest influence on the thinking of modern-day libertarians.[49]

On the other hand, there are numerous leaders and scholars with high profiles in the libertarian movement who either are very religious themselves or are actively engaged in promoting the idea that not only is there no incompatibility between this philosophy and religious belief, but it has important roots in such belief.[50]

Consider this statement by Murray N. Rothbard, who is the second most influential person after Ayn Rand within the libertarian community.[51] The statement was made in reply to the critique of an atheistically oriented libertarian, John Dentinger:

> And, in particular, is freedom for Christians? The libertarian movement, and the Libertarian Party, will get nowhere in America—or throughout the world—so long as it is perceived, as it generally is, as a movement dedicated to atheism. Nock, Morley, Chodorov, Flynn et al. were not atheists, but for various accidental reasons of history, the libertarian movement after the 1950s consisted almost exclusively of atheists. There is nothing inherently wrong with this, except that many libertarians have habitually and wrongly acted as if religious people in general and Christians in particular are pariahs and equivalent to statists. This pernicious attitude, combined with aggressive luftmenschship, has managed to turn off a huge number of middle-class Americans. . . .

In all the talk about "outreach" among libertarians, I never hear a word about outreach to Christians. In keeping with this hostility, the *only* reference John Dentinger has to Christians in his article is to the "hate-filled religious right." *Of course,* we have to strongly oppose the theocracy of the Moral Majoritarians. But the religious right is not the sum and substance of Christianity in America. And I have yet to see Dentinger (or others like him) roll out the welcome mat to libertarian-minded Christians. I think that the hostility to Ron Paul by [libertarians] such as Dentinger reflects their dim perception that the bell has tolled for the old comfortable days when libertarians were only a small group of marginal people cut off from American life. Yes, freedom is indeed for everyone, including the large number of Americans scorned by Dentinger and company, and this is precisely what they are complaining about.[52]

It is crucial, both for the health of the libertarian movement and for the promotion of simple justice, that it be realized, once and for all, that religious belief is totally compatible with the libertarian philosophy. To be sure, there have been and still are religious people who have acted in a manner contrary to libertarianism. They have initiated violence against nonaggressors. One need only point to the crusades, religious wars, inquisitions, pogroms, theocracies, and violations of the rights of authors such as Salman Rushdie. That does not mean, however, that religion is intrinsically antilibertarian. There are nonreligious people, too, who have invaded the persons or property of others. And for every believer who engages in rights violations, there are thousands who lead exemplary lives, from the libertarian point of view.

There are no insuperable barriers stopping people of religious disposition from embracing libertarianism. One can go further, and claim that all people of religious persuasion are really libertarians; at least insofar as they embrace the commandment "Thou shalt not steal."[53] This commandment makes no sense apart from the assumption of private property rights. If the individual had no rights to property, it would be impossible to steal. The commandment logically implies the existence of legitimate titles to property.

Nor does this commandment provide for exceptions. It does not say, for example, that you must not steal unless you are doing so in behalf of a government, or unless a majority vote decides in favor of the theft. The command is stark and simple. It prohibits the unconsented transfer of property from one person to another. This is all that libertarianism amounts to: a denial of the rightfulness of theft in any form, for any reason whatsoever. The entire corpus of the libertarian philosophy amounts to no more than the working out of the implications of this religiously based commandment.

Wealth and Whimsy:
Being Rich, Producing Riches

The question is: What are the theological resources of the Christian tradition for understanding the production of wealth? The answer is: Apparently there are none. *Apparently.* That is, were one to run through a hypothetical index of two millennia of Christian theology looking for entries under the category of "Wealth, production of," the findings would be pretty slim. Indeed, it is doubtful that we would find that category in our hypothetical index. Certainly it is not included in the standard dictionaries of Christian theology.

Irving Kristol was guilty of only slight hyperbole when on the dustjacket he said of Michael Novak's 1982 book *The Spirit of Democratic Capitalism,* "Incredible as it may seem, this is the first book to provide us with a critical appreciation of democratic capitalism from a theological point of view." True, in 1981 Robert Benne had published his *The Ethic of Democratic Capitalism.* The same year saw the appearance of George Gilder's *Wealth and Poverty,* which argued in what might be described as a theological mode that capitalist productivity is based upon altruism and ultimate trust. If we go back to the latter part of the nineteenth century, we find that there was a rash of Christian literature extolling what Andrew Carnegie called "the gospel of wealth." It would seem, however, that serious theological discussion of economics in relation to the production of wealth is a relatively recent development.

My purpose is to explain something of why this should be so. Another purpose is to suggest that, the index makers notwithstanding, the Christian tradition is rich in resources supportive of the production of wealth. For various and often complicated reasons, however, most Christian thinkers have not discussed those resources in connection with economics.

Something must be said about early Christian views toward the rich and riches, and about the earlier views to be found in Hebrew and Greek thought.[1] The ancient Greek word for riches, found also in the New Testament and the Septuagint version of the Hebrew scriptures, is *ploutos* (from which the word *plutocrat* is derived). Suggestively, the root is the Indo-European *pel,* which means both "to flow" and "to fill." At least etymologically, the connotation is one of dynamic movement, perhaps even of growth. In Greek usage, however, *ploutos* connoted something much more static. To be rich was to have it, rather than to be in the process of getting it—never mind producing it. *Ploutos* was a sign of a happy life lived within a stable order under the blessing of the gods.

In Homer, nobility and wealth went together. Some scholars say they were identical. The gain or loss of wealth, and hence of nobility, was in the hands of the gods, for misfortune and guilt could no more be separated than fortune and virtue. In Homer, an apparently nice thing about being rich was that one did not have to work. That changed with Hesiod, who taught that work is not shameful but honorable. He introduced an ethical condemnation of the arrogant rich who despoil the laboring peasant; the link between wealth and worth was thus no longer secure.

If the moral order was not as self-evident to Hesiod as it was to Homer, during the period from the pre-Socratics to Aristotle the entire social order was also unstable and very much in question. There was a tension between the social order and culture, between the individual and society. Experience taught that there were poor people who were cultured and rich people who were uncultured. Riches became only one way, and a very uncertain way, of seeking security against life's uncertainties. The idea of striving for wealth became prominent, but the good man might decline to so strive, seeking rather the true wealth of virtue and wisdom. In Plato and Aristotle we discover a functional view of wealth: it is a means to be used in the living of the virtuous life. Membership in the polis was determined less by one's wealth than by one's attitude toward wealth.

A suspicious attitude toward wealth, it becomes apparent, has deep classical roots. Aristotle thought moderate wealth better than great wealth, since it is easier to handle and less distracting from the important things in life. Plato went further, comparing material wealth most unfavorably with the true riches of wisdom, culture, and virtue. Some Cynics and Stoics radicalized this view by calling for the rejection of wealth altogether. *Paidea,* they taught, is possible only for the poor, since wealth and virtue are mutually exclusive. In contrast to Plato and Aristotle, their point of reference in thinking about material goods was no longer the polis but the individual. They had quite reversed the earlier Greek view of the connection between wealth and nobility. Later Stoics, perhaps predictably, came back to a more balanced view, acknowledging the advantages of being comfortably off over being penurious, while insisting that wealth was an *adiaphoron* that could be either good or bad depending on whether it was used to cultivate virtue and wisdom in harmony with the cosmic order. The judgment was now well entrenched, however, that riches are accompanied by a moral question mark.

That judgment is more ambivalent in the Hebrew scriptures, at least at the beginning. In Genesis 14 and 15, for example, the origin and increase of riches through the booty of war, dowries, and successful breeding are providentially guided. Wealth is the gift of God and a sign of his blessing (Deut. 28:1–14). In the later, prophetic, period, the moral question mark becomes much more prominent. This is undoubtedly related to a dramatic change in the sociological circumstances. Jerusalem and Samaria were now royal cities, and the prophets were agreed on the moral scandal of there being a small stratum of plutocrats in a population generally marked by severe poverty. That is the depiction offered in Isaiah, Jeremiah, Ezekiel, Amos, and Micah. The prophetic outrage was exacerbated by particular violations of covenantal fidelity such as forced labor, the enslavement of fellow countrymen, and fraud depriving widows and orphans of their rights. Isaiah in particular (5:14; 32; 33) associates riches with pride and he prophesies that the pomp and glory of Jerusalem will go down to the underworld, its wealth will be scattered like chaff, the city will stand waste and empty, and the wives of the nobility will share the lot of the poor whom they had previously despised.

The still later Wisdom literature returns, in a somewhat commonsensical vein, to a more positive assessment of wealth, even suggesting that the getting (if not the producing) of wealth is assisted by a life of virtue. Drawing on practical experience, it is observed that a man becomes rich if he is economical (Prov. 24:4), industrious (Ecclus. [Sirach] 31:3), and strong (Prov. 10:4), and if he refrains from wickedness. The benefits of wealth are security (Prov. 10:15), friends (Prov. 14:20), honor (Ecclus. 10:30), a full and happy life (Ecclus. 44:1–8), and the chance to give alms (Ecclus. 31:8, Tob. 12:8). Although tempered by this more appreciative view of riches, the prophetic critique is by no means lost. Especially prominent are warnings against the dangers of pride and of trusting in riches rather than in God. In Job and elsewhere, the question of theodicy is sharply raised—why the wicked should prosper while the righteous suffer want. During the intertestamental period, this question developed in an eschatological direction, offering the hope of a Day of the Lord in which such injustices will be righted. It is this eschatological note that dominates the New Testament understanding of riches.

In Matthew we encounter the young man who did not follow Jesus because he was attached to his great riches (Matt. 19:22), which occasions the remark that it is easier for a camel to go through the eye of a needle than for a rich man to enter the kingdom. Here and elsewhere, however, it would seem that Jesus was referring not to a class but to Everyman. The great question was whether one was attached to the present passing order or to the new order that was to come and that was, in Jesus, already proleptically present. Attachment to the present is marked by anxiety, which, in the Sermon on the Mount, is characterized as the attitude of the pagan (Matt. 6:25–32). In other words, the view of riches and every other attachment is not so much ethical as eschatological and theocentric. For instance, it is noted without comment that Joseph of Arimathea was a rich man, and in the lavish anointing at Bethany it appears that poverty had no particular religious significance: "For the poor you will have always with you, but you will not always have me" (Matt. 26:11).

In Mark and Luke there is a considerable sharpening of the critique of riches. In Luke especially, the rich are depicted as the opponents of Jesus, and there is a striking accent on the eschatological great reversal: those invited first to the feast do not share in it (Luke 14:24); the hungry are filled with good things while the rich are sent empty away (1:53); and those who abase themselves will be exalted (14:11; 18:29–30). In the parable of the sower, "the cares and riches and pleasures of life" are the "thorns" that choke the word (8:14). Zacchaeus gives half his goods to the poor and restores fourfold what he had gained wrongfully, and this is held up as an example (19:8). Repeatedly, the disciples are assured that their surrender of riches now will result in gain many times over, both in this life and in the world to come. The gospel accounts amply supply the liberation theologians of our day with a rhetoric to be employed against riches and the rich. Whether their polemic is attuned to modern economic realities, or whether their proposed remedies are faithful to the New Testament's eschatological promise, are quite other questions.[2]

In other parts of the New Testament we find a replay of the by now conventional ambivalences about wealth. In 1 Timothy, for instance, wealth seems to have no particular moral significance in itself, but the rich are strongly cautioned against putting their trust in the uncertainty of riches (6:17–19). James, on the other hand, has a vigorous polemic against the rich, apparently based on the pastoral experience of rich Christians who lorded it over the rest of the community and had no compunctions about getting richer by exploiting their poorer brethren (James 2:1–9). The distinctive turn in New Testament usage comes with Paul, and is also reflected in Revelation. Paul seems quite relaxed about what the world calls riches, suggesting almost an "easy come, easy go" attitude. Wealth does not really matter much one way or another, so long as one is not attached to it, and so long as one shares generously with those in need (2 Cor. 8:1–10).

The folly of the "wisdom" of the world (1 Cor. 1:20–21) is in failing to recognize that the wealth that really counts is the wealth of God and of life in God. References to riches in Paul apply almost invariably to God, Christ, and the Christian community. It might be said that Paul spiritualizes wealth; but it is more accurate to say that he eschatologizes wealth, and thereby radically relativizes its importance. Christ is the true *plousios* (2 Cor. 8:9); the word of God dwells "richly" in the community (Col. 3:16); and Christians are made rich through the poverty of Christ, which in the mystery of God is true wealth (Col. 1:27). For Paul, the eschatological reversal is not something just waiting to happen in the future. It is a way of living now that rejects worldly wisdom, which is prisoner to anxiety because it trusts in self and possessions rather than in God. Paul declares that, although poor, he makes many rich in the riches that really matter (2 Cor. 6:10). In this respect he is simply following Christ, who demonstrated that it is a law of life and salvation that the renunciation of one's own rights makes others rich.

Hauck and Kasch wrote, "Of every possession of earthly holding one must say that it is not wealth or security but simply an instrument in the ministry of love, with no dignity of its own. This is the substance of Paul's admonition to the Corinthians."[3] It seems that in Paul we find a kind of fulfillment of the Indo-European root of *ploutos,* which, as mentioned earlier, means "to flow" or "to fill." The wealth that matters, according to Paul, is that which flows from the riches of God through Christ and is already, in an anticipatory mode, "filled" with the glory that is to be. There are in Paul no sweated moralisms about riches or the rich. The injunction to be generous to others is emphasized, for to be anxiously grasping is to interrupt, as it were, the flow. The chief point, however, is that once one has understood the true location of riches in God, everything else falls into place.

There is in Paul what might be called an eschatological light-heartedness, even playfulness, with respect to the present order, including worldly goods. "I mean, brethren, the appointed time has grown very short; from now on, let those who have wives live as though they had none, and those who mourn as though they were not mourning, and those who rejoice as though they were not rejoicing, and those who buy as though they had no goods, and those who deal with the world as though they had no dealings with it. For the form of this world is passing away" (1 Cor. 7:29–31). However long the time may be, the Christian's way of being in the world has already been transformed. "Therefore, if any one is in Christ, he is a new creation; the old has passed away, behold, the new has come" (2 Cor. 5:17). This makes possible a kind of taunting of the world's standards. "We are treated as imposters, and yet are true; as unknown, and yet well known; as dying, and behold we live; as punished, and yet not killed; as sorrowful, yet always rejoicing; as poor, yet making many rich; as having nothing, and yet possessing everything" (2 Cor. 6:8–10).

Although taunting the world's standards, the Christian is not freed from obligations in the world; indeed he or she is freed to fulfill such obligations. This is evident in Paul's appeal to the Corinthians to give generously to help poorer brethren elsewhere. "The point is this: he who sows sparingly will also reap sparingly, and he who sows bountifully will also reap bountifully. Each one must do as he has made up his mind, not reluctantly or under compulsion, for God loves a cheerful giver." Freed from anxiety, we can dare to be generous, "because God is able to provide you with every blessing in abundance, so that you may always have enough of everything and may provide in abundance for every good work" (2 Cor. 9:6–9).

This Pauline lightheartedness about economic matters erupted persistently in subsequent Christian history; but it was as frequently suppressed by sobersided formulas for what would later be called economic justice. Many commentators have succumbed to the temptation of dismissing Paul's relative indifference to economic justice—as well as to so much else that preoccupies politicized Christianity today—as a product of an "interim ethic" that assumed the imminent return of Christ in glory. It is doubtful, however, that Paul's recommended attitude toward worldly affairs, including economics, was substantively affected by eschatological schedules. His is a way of "being in the world" that can be accepted or rejected whether history's promised consummation is five years or five millennia removed.

In the biblical and subsequent Christian literature we find persistent jeremiads against the rich and against preoccupation with riches. In the last century and this, such strictures have been conventionally interpreted in a manner hostile to the capitalist mode of producing wealth. This too would seem to miss the point of the Pauline lightheartedness. The point is that wealth—having it or producing it—really does not matter much. This point is missed both by the avaricious, who become captive to their possessions, and by religiously driven ideologues promoting designs for a just economic order. Both are in danger of attributing an ultimacy to something that is, at most, prepenultimate. Both take wealth altogether too seriously. Of course, different attitudes toward wealth usually appear in mixed form rather than as pure types. The choice of poverty in monasticism, for example, can be depicted as implying a condemnation of worldly wealth, or as exemplifying an eschatologically liberated way of life that radically relativizes the exigencies of money, and of much else.

Similarly—and contrary to many earnest arguments advanced about the connections between the Reformation and capitalism—it may be suggested that the reformers' articulation of the Pauline doctrine of grace assisted economic enterprise chiefly by underscoring the truth that worldly success does not matter that much, it does not matter ultimately. In the Calvinist tradition, economic achievement may have been motored less by its being viewed as a token of election than by the fact that a grace-based Pauline lightheartedness about worldly achievements created free space within which a variety of callings could be exercised in good conscience. The question of ultimate salvation is already attended to by the utterly gratuitous mercy of God. That being the case, Christian vocations, also in the economic realm, are no longer a desperate quest for salvation but an exercise of grace-full insouciance in response to the gift already given.

The heavy breathing of the theologizing, moralizing, and even "salvationizing" of economic matters would seem to be a later phenomenon among Christians in the Reformation traditions. It is, for instance, dramatically evident in the United States in the Social Gospel movement of the late nineteenth and early twentieth centuries. Ironically enough, it is evident in Roman Catholic liberation theology, which has embraced with enthusiasm this aspect of late Protestantism. What appears as theologized activism in the Americas frequently has its roots in European, notably German, thought. With respect to the Social Gospel, the influence of Albrecht Ritschl was enormous, and Americans continued to depend on that stream of liberalism as made more accessible by English writers such as R. H. Tawney, F. D. Maurice, and William Temple, all of whom were adamant in opposing laissez-faire capitalism.

The conscientious determination to deny to economics its sphere of freedom is evident, for instance, in John C. Bennett's *Christian Ethics and Social Policy* (1946). With respect to the themes encapsulated there, little has changed in the past half century. Bennett's earnest moralizing of the economic sphere is to be found in the latest pronouncements on economic justice by old-line Protestant churches and, increasingly, by the Roman Catholic bishops in this country. Such pronouncements typically reflect an entrenched emphasis on the distribution of wealth rather than the creation of wealth, a greater concern for the means of production than for production. Indeed, in harder versions of this approach, the Pauline view that economics does not matter much is reversed. The economic structure, "systemically analyzed," is taken to be determinative of everything else—including the allegedly illusory liberation proposed in Paul's studied indifference toward economics.

Not surprisingly, theologized economic theories have been almost invariably socialist in their direction. It is not surprising because socialism is premised upon a refusal to accept the resistance of economics to "making sense," especially theological sense. The taken-for-granted nature of this view is evident in Paul Tillich's flat assertion, "Any serious Christian must be a socialist."[4] Similarly, in the past century the maxim has been widely affirmed that socialism is the economics of which Christianity is the religion. The assumptions implicit in this viewpoint were endorsed also by neo-orthodox theologians who were on most questions vigorously opposed to the Ritschlian tradition of nineteenth-century liberalism. This was notably the case with Karl Barth, arguably the greatest Christian theologian of this century.

After World War II, when Barth was striving for an "even-handedness" between East and West, his socialism was, at least in part, a strategy for ideological accommodation. In 1950 he wrote, "Anyone who does not want communism—and none of us do—should take socialism seriously."[5] In his great *Church Dogmatics*, however, Barth leaves no doubt that the grounding of his economic views goes much deeper than mere strategic considerations.[6] Barth treats economics under the rubric of "work" and "labor" within the context of the doctrine of creation. Work is relentlessly teleological, directed toward definite ends, and this he calls the "criterion of objectivity." The question to be asked of economic activity is: "Does the ostensible worker know what he wills and will what he knows?" What Barth calls "right work" is "obedience to the divine command." This means that "all dilettante or botched work, however high and noble its purposes and however rich its material profit, cannot possibly be right and is not therefore obedience."

There is little of the Pauline lightheartedness, never mind whimsy, in Barth's understanding of work. "We are either heart and soul in a thing or we take things easily. *Tertium non datur.*" Work is to advance significantly the human condition, although he allows that a proper end of work could include "even perhaps adornments of human existence." The latter is a reluctant allowance, however. Some so-called work is nothing more than amusing others, and while Barth says he does not "grudge" people the need to make a living, he is not prepared to call "worthy and valuable work" those activities that depend upon "the stupidity and superficiality, the vanity and bad taste, the errors and vices of numerous other people."

He is certainly not prepared to describe as worthy work activity that is involved in the "almost unequivocally demonic process which consists in the amassing and multiplying of possessions expressed in financial calculations . . . i.e., the 'capital' which in the hands of the relatively few, who pull all the strings, may equally well, in a way wholly [outside] the control of the vast majority and therefore quite arbitrarily or accidentally, be a source of salvation or perdition for whole nations or generations."

In such a system work is often "completely alien" to the worker, "being performed in the service of a sinister and heartless and perpetually ambiguous idol." Capitalists who say that such a system is necessary to produce wealth and provide jobs must be told that their claim is unacceptable. If they cannot change the system, "then the question is to be addressed the more acutely to the state, to the government or Parliament, whether it is in fact politically possible or legitimate to allow the so-called economy to be administered in this free, or rather ineffectual, manner." If the politicians are unresponsive, then appeal must be made to "the whole of human society," for "in the last analysis, it is society which has to grant work and define its aims." In the absence of clearly determined ends, "meaningless and nonsensical and worthless work constantly increases." Since it is possible that the great mass of employees view their work "in what is at bottom a 'capitalistic' or unthinking way in relation to the question of ends," it is not surprising that the owners and employers take advantage of that mindlessness.

Work must therefore be objective, that is, directed to proper ends, and worthy of human beings. It must also be "human work" in the sense that it is "a social act involving association and comradeship." The vital claims of workers are fulfilled only if their work is "co-ordinated" with that of others. Some work may be done in happy and innocent freedom from this concern for co-ordination, but that is the rare exception. There are those who lift up the delights and benefits of competition, as though work were a contest in which the best receives the prize, but they forget that "*the sphere of human work is not a playing field*" (emphasis added). Economic competition becomes a deadly contest in which "the reward is no more and no less than existence itself." "Hence there is no fun in this contest." Against such contest there must be a countermovement of setting limits on economic freedom and "where the command of God is heard it will always be a summons to counter-movements of this kind."

In Barth's bleak view, work "under the sign of competition" sets one man against the other "with force and cunning, and there cannot fail to be innumerable prisoners, wounded and dead." Because of the unjust distribution of the ownership of the means of production, "it can hardly be denied that on the whole, at least in the West, the modern industrial process does in fact rest on the principle of the exploitation of some by others." Barth wants to make clear that he has no illusions about the solution proposed by the socialisms of the East. What he describes as "state socialism" might turn out to be "only a new and perhaps even crasser form of the oppression and exploitation of man by man." But for those in the West who live under the prevailing capitalist system it is necessary "to assert the command of God in face of this form, and to keep to the 'left' in opposition to its champions, i.e., to confess that [we are] fundamentally on the side of the victims of this disorder and to espouse their cause." Barth says the church should not "identify its message" with any economic directions, but a little later he declares, "The Christian community both can and should espouse the cause of this or that branch of social progress or even socialism in the form most helpful at a specific time and place and in a specific situation."

The essentially socialist Barth declares that work must be objectively directed to ends, must be worthy, must be humanly coordinated, and must, in addition, be reflective and limited. It is on the last score that we encounter a break from the earlier assertion that the sphere of human work is not a playing field. In discussing the limits of work, Barth emphasizes that the worth of a human being is not exhaustively defined by his work, and he reflects especially on the dignity of the old, the sick, and the disabled. For all of us there is a need for the "Sabbath rest" from work, which we can undertake with good conscience, for we know that "God is in charge." This quite different view of work is elaborated in an extended note worthy of quotation:

Outward and inward work will be done with more rather than less seriousness once a man realises that what he desires and does and achieves thereby, when measured by the work of God which it may attest, cannot be anything but play, i.e., a child-like imitation and reflection of the fatherly action of God which as such is a true and proper action. When children play properly, of course, they do so with supreme seriousness and devotion. Even in play, if a man does not really play properly, he is a spoilsport. We are summoned to play properly. But we must not imagine that what we desire and are able to do is more than play. Human work would certainly not be worse done, but both individually and as a whole it would be done much better, if it were not done with the frightful seriousness which is so often bestowed upon it just because fundamentally we do not think that we have to take God seriously, and therefore we must take ourselves the more terribly seriously, this usually being the surest way to invoke the spirit of idleness and sloth by way of compensation.

In that aside, a wiser Barth (or so I would suggest) would seem to be taking back much of what he had earlier urged with such "frightful seriousness." Here we detect the working out of a Pauline lightheartedness more in accord with Barth's more usual way of radically relativizing the pretensions of the present time's sweated exigencies. There is a necessary whimsy in the living of the Christian life, since we know that "God is in charge," and we are by no means sure what he is up to in the contingencies of history. While the gravamen of Barth's discussion excludes whimsy from the consideration of wealth, it is featured very prominently in his understanding of human creativity in other spheres. His treatment of Mozart is an outstanding case in point.

The creative order, says Barth, is ambiguous, containing a yes and a no, but we are not always able to sort out the positive from the negative. But no matter. "If God Himself has comprehended creation in its totality and made it His own in His Son, it is for us to acquiesce without thinking that we know better, without complaints, reproach or dismay." And here, in a longish but moving aside, he reflects on Mozart:

Why is it that this man is so incomparable? Why is it that for the receptive he has produced in almost every bar he conceived and composed a type of music for which "beautiful" is not a fitting epithet: music which for the true Christian is not mere entertainment, enjoyment or edification but food and drink. . . . Why is it possible to hold that Mozart has a place in theology, especially in the doctrine of creation and also in eschatology, although he was not a father of the Church, does not seem to have been a particularly active Christian, and was a Roman Catholic, apparently leading what might appear to us a rather frivolous existence when not occupied in his work? It is possible to give him this position because he knew something about creation in its total goodness that neither the real fathers of the Church nor our Reformers, neither the orthodox nor Liberals, neither the exponents of natural theology nor those heavily armed with the "Word of God," and certainly not the Existentialists, nor indeed any other great musicians before and after him, either know or can express as he did. . . . In the face of the problem of theodicy, Mozart had the peace of God which far transcends all the critical or speculative reason that praises and reproves. This problem lay behind him. Why then concern himself with it? He had heard, and causes those who have ears to hear, even today, what we shall not see until the end of time—the whole context of providence. . . . He heard concretely and therefore his compositions were and are total music. Hearing creation unresentfully and impartially, he did not produce merely his own music but that of creation, its twofold and yet harmonious praise of God. . . . He was remarkably free from the mania for self-expression. He simply offered himself as the agent by which little bits of horn, metal, and catgut could serve as the voices of creation, sometimes leading, sometimes accompanying and sometimes in harmony. . . . Mozart causes us to hear that even on the [negative] side, and therefore in its totality, creation praises its Master and is therefore perfect. . . . Mozart has thus created order for those who have ears to hear, and he has done it better than any scientific deduction could. This is the point which I wish to make.

And the point that I wish to make is, quite simply, that Barth's discussion of work and the economy in the fourth volume of his treatment of creation would be much more persuasive had he brought it into closer conversation with what he says about Mozart and creation in the third volume. Barth depicts Mozart as an exemplar of Pauline lightheartedness who dared to act upon the knowledge that "God is in charge," whose creativity is theocentric and eschatological, which is to say it is freed from the teleological calculations of social utility. This, one might suggest, is the freedom that Barth should more clearly have related to the economic sphere in connection with the creativity that is essential for the production of wealth. Barth was not willing to extend to economic creativity the wonder that he accorded to aesthetic creativity. He readily acknowledged a "hidden hand" in Mozart's work, but not in the work of others that might equally bear witness to the goodness of creation.

The connections that Barth does not explore are suggestively developed by another theological giant of this century, Dietrich Bonhoeffer.[7] His view of human creativity, also in the economic sphere, is not only theocentric but insistently Christocentric. Our labor is not a creation out of nothing, like God's creation, but "a making of new things on the basis of the creation by God. . . . The first creation of Cain was the city, the earthly counterpart of the eternal city of God. There follows the invention of fiddles and flutes, which afford to us on earth a foretaste of the music of heaven." The extraction and processing of metals, the building of homes, and all our other activities are, whether we know it or not, a readying of the world for the coming of Christ. "Through the divine mandate of labour there is to come into being a world which, knowingly or not, is waiting for Christ, is designed for Christ, is open to Christ, serves Him and glorifies Him." Although all this is under the sign of Cain, it has nonetheless been redeemed. For the Christian, the shadowed side is, as Barth said of Mozart, "behind him."

This confident, playful participation in creation, says Bonhoeffer, has its own integrity and freedom that must be protected, especially by the government and from the government. "Government maintains created things in their proper order, but it cannot itself engender life; it is not creative." People are creative in carrying out the divine mandates in labor, family, and the community of faith. Government is not the subject or originator of these fields of human endeavor. "If it asserts its authority beyond the limits of its assigned task it will in the long run forfeit its genuine authority over these fields." Bonhoeffer, who was executed by the Nazis in 1945, understood the danger of the totalitarian temptation to have the state impose coordination (*Gleichschaltung*) upon the society. Against the claim of the state to represent, indeed to be identical with, the people, Bonhoeffer asserts that "in Scripture there is no special commission of God for the people." The Christian knows, says Bonhoeffer, "that the people grows from below, but that government is instituted from above." Creativity, growth, a serendipitous discovery of possibilities—all of these are exercised in the arena of freedom that is from below, from the actions and interactions of free persons who are, knowingly or not, participating in God's continuing creation.

Other formative Christian theologians of this century have seemed to share Bonhoeffer's understanding of the fortuitous nature of economic growth and well-being. A recent and generally sympathetic study of John Courtney Murray chides him for having had little to say about economic justice, a subject that has become theologically de rigueur in the past three decades of Christian-Marxist dialogue and liberation theology.[8] One suspects that Murray did not spend much time on economic justice because he was not sure what it meant, and that he offered no prescriptions for the creation of wealth because he knew none, other than abiding by the restraints inherent in what he called "the American experiment in ordered liberty."

Reinhold Niebuhr, on the other hand, had a very thoroughly developed theology of socialist economics in his earlier years.[9] In his mature years he abandoned his socialist enthusiasms and expressed grudging admiration for the productivity of economic liberalism. It seems, however, that neither Murray nor Niebuhr was tempted to write a theology of economics—Murray because it seemed quite unnecessary, and Niebuhr because in that effort he was once burned and twice shy. Economics, one might suggest, appears as the dismal science precisely because it is in such stark contrast to the freedom of economic activity, which is anything but dismal. Efforts to theologize economics tend to produce dismal theology.

Economics, like some other aspects of life, is too important to be taken seriously. At least one should be careful about taking it with theological seriousness. A theologically informed appreciation of economic life and the production of wealth should be marked by a sense of whimsy and wonder in the face of the fortuitous, contingent, chancy, and unpredictable realities of economic behavior. Such an appreciation will have less to do with Karl Barth's criteria of economic justice and more with what Johan Huizinga describes as "Homo ludens."[10] To suggest such a connection between wealth and whimsy, between productivity and playfulness, is not to say that economics is of little consequence or unworthy of our attention. Intelligent playfulness, however, is only made possible by faith; just as Pauline lightheartedness is only thinkable on the far side of the cross, and just as Mozart could do what he did only because the intimidating anxieties about ultimate rights and wrongs were, by the grace of God, behind him.

The economic sphere is a playing field, after all. Jeremiads against pride, greed, and avarice will always be in order. People can take the game too seriously, just as the Mets can take the pennant too seriously and lose both the pleasure of playing and the pennant. Of course, at the time it is being played, the game may be totally engrossing and almost painfully earnest. If the game is not to consume the entirety of one's life, its time must be limited by other times; this is the profound wisdom of the Sabbath rest. Any game, including economics, can become an idol to which we surrender our existence, at which point it ceases to be a game. This truth applies as well to the wealthy stockbroker as to the overly earnest small entrepreneur, and to the poor campesino who resigns himself to what he believes to be his economic fate. In each case, the tragedy is that the game has become a god.

Theologians and preachers should be in the business of urging people to play fairly, but should not presume to claim any privileged knowledge about rules of economic fairness that are not derived from the general virtues for living decently. Above all, players need to be reminded that it is only a game, albeit an essential game. Christian theology, one may conclude, says the most important things about economics when it is not trying to make sense out of economics. Barth, for example, writes most wisely about economics when he is writing about Mozart. Opening a new pizza parlor, designing a new widget, or manufacturing a better automobile are all somebody's Violin Concerto in D Major. It may not be our idea of Mozart, but then the people doing those things didn't ask our opinion. If we asked theirs, we might discover that they do not think too highly of people who write essays such as this, either. If we are not moved to applaud one another's enterprises, we can at least refrain from jeering, and wish one another well with the diverse games on which we all depend—we more obviously on theirs than they on ours.

NOTES

ONE   EARLY CHRISTIANITY AND THE CREATION OF CAPITAL

The author offers special thanks to Dr. George B. Baldwin of the World Bank in Washington (retired).

1. Xenophon *Oeconomicus* 1.4, etc.; Cicero *On Duties* 2.87.

2. Hesiod *Works and Days* 303–4, 381–2.

3. This huge debt, equivalent to 240 million sesterces, is what an Egyptian king owed to Roman bankers; they insisted on naming their own treasurer of Egypt so they could collect. Cicero *For Rabirius* 21–22.28.

4. Or perhaps by reducing padded figures to the correct amounts; reference from Professor Gilles Quispel of Utrecht (retired).

5. D. E. Oakman, in *Jesus and the Economic Problems of His Day* (Lewiston, N.Y.: Mellen, 1986), p. 171 n. 22, refrains from discussing this parable, "a commentary on conventional behavior in the early empire."

6. *Satires* 6.75–79, trans. J. R. Jenkinson, *Persius: The Satires* (Warminster, England: Aris & Phillips, 1980), pp. 69–61. Persius had 2 million according to Suetonius *Life of Aulus Persius Flaccus* (Loeb Library, 2.496).

7. *Satires* 3.69 (Jenkinson, *Persius,* p. 35).

8. B. T. D. Smith, *The Parables of the Synoptic Gospels* (Cambridge: Cambridge University Press, 1937), p. 143.

9. Ibid., p. 194.

10. H. Gressmann, *Vom reichen Mann und armen Lazarus* (Abhandlungen der königlich preussischen Akademie der Wissenschaften [Berlin], 1918, Philosophisch-historische Klasse, No. 7).

11. Note that Acts 5:4 contradicts this picture.

12. K. Lake, "The Communism of Acts II and IV–VI," in *The Beginnings of Christianity Part I*, ed. F. J. F. Jackson and K. Lake (New York: Macmillan, 1933), 5:140–51.

13. H. Conzelmann, *Die Apostelgeschichte* (Tübingen: Mohr, 1963), p. 31.

14. Josephus *Antiquities* 15.371.

15. Lucian *Peregrinus* 13.

16. R. Duncan-Jones, *The Economy of the Roman Empire: Quantitative Studies* (Cambridge: Cambridge University Press, 1974), pp. 343–44; cf. T. Frank, *Economic Survey of Ancient Rome* (Baltimore: Johns Hopkins University Press, 1933–1940), 1:387–402, 5:22–29.

17. Plutarch *Crassus* 2.2. We may call a sestertius a dollar, with a grape picker getting four a day—that is, one denarius (Matt. 20:2).

18. Ibid. 2.3–7.

19. Seneca *On Clemency* 1.15.

20. Pliny *Natural History* 18.37.

21. Tacitus *Annals* 2.37–38.

22. Suetonius *Tiberius* 49.1: *census maximus fuit*.

23. Seneca *On Benefits* 2.27.

24. Pliny *Natural History* 9.117–18; Tacitus *Annals* 12.22, 14.12; Dio Cassius 60.32.

25. Dio Cassius 6.34.4; Pliny *Natural History* 33.134.

26. His brother Felix was prefect of Judaea (Acts 23–24).

27. Tacitus *Annals* 12.53; cf. Pliny *Epistles* 7.29.2, 8.6.

28. Tacitus *Annals* 13.14; S. I. Oost, "The Career of M. Antonius Pallas," *American Journal of Philology* (1958), pp. 113–39.

29. Tacitus *Annals* 12.53; Dio Cassius 62.14.38; ("400 million"); Pliny *Natural History* 33.134.

30. Seneca *Epistles* 119.9, 120.19; Pliny *Natural History* 33.134.

31. Plutarch *Life of Publicola* 15.3 (twelve thousand talents).

32. Pliny *Natural History* 33.135.

33. Ibid. 29.7–8.

34. Petronius 45, 71, 76, 88, 117; Duncan-Jones, *Economy of the Roman Empire*, p. 241.

35. Pliny *Natural History* 29.9.

36. Suetonius *On Grammarians* 23; the yield is less than what the Christian Papias expected in the coming reign of God.

37. Petronius 71, 74, 75, 77.

38. Seneca *Epistles* 87.16, 90.38–39.

39. Ibid. 119.9.

40. Ibid. 101.2, 4; compare the rich fool of Luke 12:16–20.

41. Seneca *Epistles* 14.55, 13.30, 3.30.

42. Ibid. 77.1–4.

43. Frank, *Economic Survey,* 2.38–56 (Papyrus Bouriant 42 of the year 167 lists the "estate of Seneca" under "estates of Titus").

44. Dio Cassius 62.2.1.

45. Seneca *Epistles* 41.7.

46. Tacitus *Annals* 6.33.

47. Martial 3.31: *et servit dominae numerosus debitor arcae.*

48. Petronius 53: *collocari* and *in arcam.*

49. Duncan-Jones, *Economy of the Roman Empire,* pp. 20–32.

50. Pliny *Epistles* 3.19.4, 8.

51. Martial 4.37.

52. Seneca *To Helvia* 10.9; Martial, who had much less money than Seneca, says Gavius Apicius spent seventy million (3.22).

53. Tacitus *Annals* 13.42; Dio Cassius 61.10.3, 62.25.3.

54. Frank Beare, *The Epistle to the Philippians,* 3d ed., (London: Black, 1973), p. 110, quoting Aristotle *Nicomachean Ethics,* 5.4.13, 1132b11–16.

55. Hermas *Visions* 3.6.5, 10.1.4; *Mandates* 3.5, 8.10; *Similitudes* 1.6, 1.10–11, 2.5.

56. Irenaeus *Against Heresies* 4.30.1.

57. Clement *Who Is the Rich Man Being Saved?* 26.3, 31.6, 14.1.

58. Quoted in Nigel Harris, *Beliefs in Society* (Penguin: Harmondsworth, England, 1971), p. 206.

59. Callistus at Rome (Hippolytus *Refutation* 9.12); Paul of Samosata at Antioch (Eusebius *Church History* 7.30.7); Maximus at Alexandria (*The Amherst Papyri* I 3[a]); cf. R. Bogaert, "Changeurs et banquiers chez les pères de l'église," Ancient Society 4 (1973), pp. 239–70.

60. Pliny *Epistles* 10.96; Tertullian *To Scapula* 4.7.

61. Eusebius *Church History* 5.18.11.

62. See my *Early Christianity and Society* (San Francisco: Harper & Row, 1977), pp. 96–123.

63. Clement of Alexandria *Miscellanies* 3.6–9.

64. M. I. Finley, *The Ancient Economy* (Berkeley: University of California Press, 1973), p. 144.

65. T. F. Divine, "Usury," in *New Catholic Encyclopedia* (New York: McGraw-Hill, 1967), 14:499.

66. M. Weber, *The Protestant Ethic and the Spirit of Capitalism*, trans. Talcott Parsons (London: Unwin, 1930); E. Troeltsch, *The Social Teaching of the Christian Churches* (New York: Macmillan, 1931).

67. Troeltsch, *Social Teaching,* pp. 609–10.

68. Ibid., pp. 644–45.

TWO   ECONOMICS AND JUSTICE: A JEWISH EXAMPLE

All translations, unless otherwise noted, are by the author.

1. The distinction between distributive and rectifying justice is, of course, based on Aristotle *Nicomachean Ethics* bk. 5, 1130b30ff. However, one does not find in Aristotle, either here or in the *Politics,* criteria of justice pertaining to production. Production seems to have been for slaves, hence beneath the level at which true political justice applies (1134a25). Money making, like slavery, was seen as something done "under constraint" (*biaios,* 1096a5), hence interfering with the leisure needed for a life of practical, let alone intellectual, excellence. See 1171b1; see also *Politics* 1278a1, 1325a25, 1328b35ff.; M. I. Finley, "Aristotle and Economic Analysis" in *Articles on Aristotle,* vol. 2: *Ethics and Politics,* eds. J. Barnes, M. Schofield, and P. Sorabji (New York: St. Martin's Press, 1977), pp. 148ff. Cf. Michael Novak, "Productivity and Social Justice" in *Will Capitalism Survive?* ed. E. W. Lefever (Washington, D.C.: Ethics and Public Policy Center, 1979), pp. 34–35.

2. See Karl Marx, *The Essential Writings,* ed. and trans. F. L. Bender (New York: Harper Torchbooks, 1972), pp. 86ff.

3. See Aristotle *Nicomachean Ethics,* 1131a6.

4. See Gabriel Marcel, *Being and Having,* trans. K. Farrer (New York: Harper Torchbooks, 1965), p. 132. Max Weber argued that the separation of the workplace from the home is an important precondition for the emergence of capitalism. See *The Protestant Ethic and the Spirit of Capitalism,* trans. T. Parsons (New York: Scribner's, 1958), pp. 21–22.

5. See *Mishnah* (hereafter *"M."*) 'Abot 1.10; and *'Abot deRabbi Nathan,* ed. Schechter (New York: n.p., 1945), version A, chap. 11.

6. That is why before any benefit from worldly things may be enjoyed, God must first be praised to emphasize that "the earth is the

Lord's" (Ps. 24:1). See *Talmud Yerushalmi / Palestinian Talmud* (hereafter "*Y.*") Berakhot 6.1/9d.

7. See Philo *De Specialibus Legibus* 2.62; see also Josephus *Contra Apionem* 2.175, *Antiquities* 16.43.

8. The rabbis note that Scripture stigmatizes the man who voluntarily extends his indenture beyond six years (Exod. 21:6) because he is "removing from himself the yoke of God and causing the yoke of flesh and blood to rule over him." *Tosefta* (hereafter "*T.*") Baba Kama 7.5; see also *Babylonian Talmud* (hereafter "*B.*") Kiddushin 22b.

9. See *'Abot deRabbi Nathan*, version A, chap. 11; see also *M.* Ketubot 5.5.

10. *Mishneh Torah* (hereafter "*MT*") Hilkhot Mattnot 'Aniyyim, 10.7 re Lev. 25:35; see also *B.* Shabbat 118a.

11. Thus, for example, the commandment to honor one's parents includes caring for their bodily needs; that care is to be administered out of the parents' own funds. Only if they are destitute are they to become the objects of charity like anyone else in poverty. See *B.* Kiddushin 32a; *Tosafot* (hereafter "*Tos.*") s.v. "oru" re *B.* Ketubot 49b and *Y.* Kiddushin 1.7/61c.

12. See *B.* Sanhedrin 20b.

13. Regarding general rabbinic suspicion of those in political power, see, e.g., *M.* 'Abot 1.10, 2.3.

14. See Friedrich A. Hayek, *The Road to Serfdom* (Chicago: University of Chicago Press, 1954), pp. 140ff.

15. For a discussion of the various biblical terms for poverty and their meanings, see *Vayiqra Rabbah* 34.6.

16. See *Sifra:* Behar re Lev. 25:39, ed. Weiss (Vienna: Schlessinger, 1862), 109c; Maimonides, *MT:* Hilkhot 'Abadaim, 1.1.

17. *M.* Shebi'it 10.3.

18. *M.* Shebi'it 10.4. See *B.:* Gittin 36a.

19. *B.* Gittin 36b. For Samuel's solution to the problem of the sabbatical year and loans, one involving prior negotiation between borrower and lender without intervening court action, see *B.* Makkot 3B; see also *Responsa Ha-R'osh*, ed. Venice (1552), 77.2. For earlier nonlegal approaches to the same problem, see *M.* Shebi'it 10.8–9.

20. *B.* Gittin 36b.

21. *M.* Gittin 4.3.

22. Ludwig Blau, "Prosbul im Lichte der Griechischen Papyri und der Rechtsgeschichte," in *Festschrift zum 50jaehrigen Bestehen der Franz-Josef-Landesrabbinerschule in Budapest*, ed. L. Blau (Budapest, 1927), pp. 96ff.

See Louis Ginzberg, "The Significance of the Halachah for Jewish History," trans. A. Hertzberg, in *On Jewish Law and Lore* (Philadelphia: Jewish Publication Society of America, 1955), pp. 79ff.

23. Isaac Weiss, *Dor Dor ve-Dorshav* (Vilna: Romm, 1904), 1:163. See also Karo, *Kesef Mishneh* on Maimonides, *MT:* Hilkhot Mamrim, 2.2; *Maharam Schiff* on B. Gittin 36a.

24. *B.* Gittin 36b–37a. See Blau, "Prosbul," in *Festschrift,* pp. 112ff.

25. Chanoch Albeck, *Commentary on the Mishnah* (Heb.): Zera'im (Jerusalem: Bialik Institute, 1957), addenda, p. 383; David Halivni, *Meqorot u-Mesorot:* Nashim (Tel Aviv: Ovir, 1968), p. 539, n. 1.

26. Even long after the jubilee system had ceased to be in operation, the sale of an ancestral portion of land was considered morally reprehensible. See *Y.* Ketubot 2.10/26d and *Y.* Kiddushin 1.5/60c.

27. See *B.* 'Arakhin 32b re Lev. 25:10.

28. *B.* Gittin 36a–b; *Y.* Gittin 4.3/45c–d. See *B.* Kiddushin 38b and *Tos.,* s.v. "hashmattat kesafim."

29. *B.* Gittin 36b.

30. See, e.g., *B.* Pesahim 116b; see also *Responsa Ha-Ritba,* no. 97, ed. Kafih (Jerusalem: Mosad Harav Kook, 1959), pp. 114–15.

31. See *B.* Berakhot 19b re Prov. 21:30; *Y.* Ta'anit 2.4/65d.

32. See *B.* Sanhedrin 21b re Deut. 17:16–17; *Bemidbar Rabbah* 19.1.

33. See *B.* Gittin 14a and parallels.

34. See *M.* 'Eduyot 1.5.

35. For the human reconstitution of the original Covenant in the postexilic Second Jewish Commonwealth, see Neh. 10:1ff.

36. See, e.g., *B.* 'Abodah Zarah 36b; Maimonides, *MT:* Hilkhot Mamrim, 2.1ff.

37. *B.* Gittin 36b; *Tos.,* s.v. "ve-tiqqun rabbanan." Also, rabbinic sources indicate that the additional taxes imposed by the Roman occupiers of Palestine made observance of the sabbatical year much more difficult. See *Vayiqra Rabbah* 1.1 re Ps. 103:20, ed. Margulies (Jerusalem: Israel Ministry of Culture and Education, 1953), 1:4–5.

38. See *M.* Nega'im 12.5 re Lev. 14:36; *Sifra:* Metzora, ed. Weiss, 73a; see also *T.* 'Arakhin 4.24.

39. See *Y.* Berakhot 6.1/10a; *B.* Ketubot 111b re Ps. 72:16; *Ber'esheet Rabbah* 15.7 re Job 28:5, ed. Theodor/Albeck (Jerusalem: Wahrmann, 1965), 1:139.

40. Adam Smith, *The Wealth of Nations* (New York: Modern Library, 1937), p. 423.

41. See *B.* Yoma 69b.

42. *M.* Shebi'it 10.2.

43. *Y.* Shebi'it 10.2/39c. See *T.* Shebi'it 8.6 and Saul Lieberman, *Tosefta Kifshuta:* Zera'im (New York: Jewish Theological Seminary of America, 1955), p. 587.

44. See *B.* Shebu'ot 47b and Rabbenu Asher (R'osh), *Gittin,* 4.17. Cf. Maimonides, *MT:* Hilkhot Shemittah ve-Yobel, 9.14 and Karo, *Kesef Mishneh* thereon.

45. For the legal differences between real estate (*qarqa'ot*) and movable things (*metaltalin*), and the ancient priority of the former over the latter, see *M.* Kiddushin 1.5; *B.* Kiddushin 26a–b; I. H. Herzog, *The Main Institutions of Jewish Law,* 2d ed. (London and New York: Soncino, 1965), 1:99ff.

46. Of course, the high standards of the Covenant were frequently violated in practice. See, e.g., 2 Kings 4:1; Jer. 34:8ff.; Amos 2:8; Job 22:6. However, such violation does not prove the thesis of Max Weber (following earlier Bible critics) that the Torah's legislation in these areas is "utopian." Cf. *Ancient Judaism,* ed. and trans. H. H. Gerth and D. Martindale (Glencoe, Ill.: Free Press, 1952), p. 68.

47. *Y.* Shebi'it 10.2/39c; see also *Sifre:* Debarim, no. 113, ed. Finkelstein (New York: Jewish Theological Seminary of America, 1969), p. 173.

48. *Y.* Shebi't 10.2/39c; *Sifre:* Debarim, 173. See Maimonides, *MT:* Hilkhot Shemittah ve-Yobel, 9.15–16. The Babylonian sources, on the other hand, do not make this connection. See *B.* Makkot 3b; *Tos.,* s.v. "ha-moser." That is why the Babylonian sources have the tendency to see the *prosbul* as far more radical than the Palestinian sources do. See *B.* Gittin 36b re Ezra 10:8; Halivni, *Meqorot u-Mesorot.*

49. Rabbenu Nissim Gerondi (Ran) on Alfasi, *Gittin,* chap. 4, ed. Vilna, 18b–19a; Meiri, *Bet Ha-Behirah:* Gittin, ed. Schulsinger (Jerusalem: Israeli Talmud Institute, 1972), p. 155. Regarding the important function of legal fictions: "When a new juridical form arises it is joined directly on to an old and existing institution and in this way the certainty and development of the old is procured for the new. This is the notion of Fiction, which was of the greatest importance in the development of Roman Law and which has often been laughably misunderstood by moderns." Friedrich Karl von Savigny, *Vom Beruf unserer Zeit fuer Gesetzgebung und Rechtswissenschaft,* 2d ed. (1828), p. 32, translated and quoted by Lon L. Fuller, *Legal Fictions* (Stanford, Calif.: Stanford University Press, 1967), p. 59. See J. T. Noonan, Jr., *The Scholastic Analysis of Usury* (Cambridge, Mass.: Harvard University Press, 1957), pp. 200–201 and passim.

50. Maimonides, *MT:* Hilkhot Melakhim, 11.1ff., emphasizes that even in the time of the Messiah, the law will remain binding in all its specifics—and a fortiori before the Messiah comes!

THREE   WEALTH AND VIRTUE: THE DEVELOPMENT OF CHRISTIAN
ECONOMIC TEACHING

1. Kristol notes that

the terms "prophetic" and "rabbinic," which come of course from the Jewish tradition, indicate the two poles within which the Jewish tradition operates. They are not two equal poles: The rabbinic is always the stronger. In an Orthodox Hebrew school, the prophets are read only by those who are far advanced. The rest of the students read the first five books of the Bible, and no more. They learn the Law. The prophets are only for people who are advanced in their learning and not likely to be misled by prophetic fever.

Orthodox Jews have never despised business; Christians have. The act of commerce, the existence of a commercial society, has always been a problem for Christians. Commerce has never been much of a problem for Jews. I have never met an Orthodox Jew who despised business—though I have met some Reformed Jews who are businessmen and despise business.

Getting rich has never been regarded as being in any way sinful, degrading, or morally dubious within the Jewish religion, so long as such wealth is acquired legally and used responsibly. . . . It was generally assumed that the spirit of commerce is perfectly compatible with full religious faith and full religious practice. I think this is true in Islam as well, but it is not true in Christianity. The difference is that both Islam and Judaism are religions of the Law, and Christianity is a religion that repeals the Law. This difference gives Christianity certain immense advantages over both Judaism and Islam in terms of spiritual energy; but in its application to the practical world, it creates enormous problems.

Irving Kristol, "Christianity, Judaism, and Socialism," chap. 29 in *Reflections of a Neoconservative: Looking Back, Looking Ahead* (New York: Basic Books, 1983), pp. 316–17. For an account of economics within the framework of Jewish law and morality, see Meir Tamari, *With All Your Possessions: Jewish Ethics and Economic Life* (New York: Free Press, 1987).

2. "I will insist," wrote John Adams in 1809, "that the Hebrews have done more to civilize men than any other nation. If I were an athe-

ist, and believed in blind eternal fate, I should still believe that fate had ordained the Jews to be the most essential instrument for civilizing the nations. If I were an atheist of the other sect, who believe or pretend to believe that all is ordered by chance, I should believe that chance had ordered the Jews to preserve and propagate to all mankind the doctrine of a supreme, intelligent, wise, almighty sovereign of the universe, which I believe to be the great essential principle of all morality, and consequently of all civilization." *The Works of John Adams,* ed. C. F. Adams (Boston: Little, Brown, 1854), 9: 609–10.

3. "It is obvious," wrote Joseph Schumpeter, "that there would be no point in looking for 'economics' in the sacred writings themselves. The opinions on economic subjects that we might find—such as that believers should sell what they have and give it to the poor, or that they should lend without expecting anything (possibly not even repayment) from it—are ideal imperatives that form part of a general scheme of life and express this general scheme and nothing else, least of all scientific propositions." *History of Economic Analysis,* edited from manuscript by Elizabeth Boody Schumpeter (New York: Oxford University Press, 1954), 71.

4. See Michael Slattery, "The Catholic Origins of Capitalism," *Crisis* 6, no. 4 (1988): 24–29. See also Leo Moulin, *L'Aventure européenne* (Brussels: De Tempel, 1972), chaps. 4–7; Alan MacFarlane, *The Culture of Capitalism* (New York: Basil Blackwell, 1987), reviewed by Leonard P. Liggio in *Crisis* 6, no. 5 (1988): 55–56.

5. See, e.g., Adam Smith, *An Inquiry into the Nature and Causes of the Wealth of Nations,* 2 vols., ed. by R. H. Campbell and A. S. Skinner (Indianapolis: Liberty Classics, 1976), I.xi.c, I.xi.i, and III.ii.

6. See Adam Smith on the evils to which the "popular notion" that "wealth consists in money, or in gold and silver" can lead, in *Wealth of Nations,* IV.i (pp. 429–51).

7. "Of Commerce" in David Hume, *Essays Moral, Political, and Literary,* ed. Eugene F. Miller, revised edition (Indianapolis: Liberty Classics, 1987), p. 258.

8. "Of Avarice," ibid., pp. 569–73.

9. Jacques Leclercq has remarked that in the premodern period "property was essentially landed property," that is, close to nature. But "with the growth of technology, nature's contribution becomes restricted to supplying the raw materials for man's industry, which has discovered a large number of raw materials unknown to the ancients. More and more of the materials used by man for food and clothing are

finished products, very different from natural products, such as fertilizers, tinned fruit and vegetables, and nylon fabrics. In other words, the materials employed by man in his daily life are coming to depend more and more on his labour: natural products are gradually displaced by man-made products. It is no longer felt that man merely enjoys the fruits of the earth bestowed on him by God: it seems as if man himself were the author or the creator, or at least the agent, of his own well-being." *Christianity and Money,* trans. Eric Earnshaw Smith (New York: Hawthorn Books, 1960), pp. 98–99.

10. See Norman Cohn, *The Pursuit of the Millennium,* rev. ed. (Oxford: Oxford University Press, 1970).

11. See Paul Johnson, "Has Capitalism a Future?" in *Will Capitalism Survive: A Challenge by Paul Johnson with Twelve Responses,* ed. Ernest W. Lefever (Washington, D.C.: Ethics and Public Policy Center, 1976), p. 5.

12. "In Montesquieu's analysis, it was the Christian Schoolmen, not the commercial practices they condemned, that deserved the label 'criminal.' In condemning something 'naturally permitted or necessary,' the doctrinaire and unworldly Scholastics set in train a series of misfortunes, most immediately for the Jews, more generally for Europe." Ralph Lerner, *The Thinking Revolutionary: Principle and Practice in the New Republic* (Ithaca, New York: Cornell University Press, 1987), p. 204, referring to Montesquieu, *The Spirit of the Laws,* bk. 21, chap. 20.

13. See Colin McEvedy and Richard Jones, *Atlas of World Population History* (New York: Penguin Books, 1980), pp. 18, 342.

14. See Geoffrey Bibby, *Four Thousand Years Ago: A World Panorama of Life in the Second Millennium B.C.* (New York: Alfred A. Knopf, 1962), chaps. 4, 13, and 14.

15. See MacFarlane, *Culture of Capitalism.*

16. See Lester K. Little, *Religious Poverty and the Profit Economy in Medieval Europe* (Ithaca, New York: Cornell University Press, 1978), pt. 4, "The Formation of an Urban Spirituality."

17. See Alejandro A. Chafuen, *Christians for Freedom: Late-Scholastic Economics* (San Francisco: Ignatius, 1986). In chapter 6, "Commerce, Merchants and Tradesmen," Chafuen notes that by the time of the Schoolmen, "commerce had long been held in low esteem by moralists of different countries, ages and backgrounds," and he suggests that the late Scholastics took two significant forward steps; first, they "found commercial activities to be morally indifferent," that is, not evil as thought previously, and they then "outlined the advantages of commerce" for society (p. 87).

18. "Of Commerce," in Hume, *Essays*, p. 257.

19. John Locke, *Some Considerations of the Consequences of Lowering the Interest and Raising the Value of Money*, in *The Works of John Locke in Ten Volumes* (London, 1823), 5:13.

20. "By demonstrating that moral distinctions are matters of sentiment, Hume had, at a single stroke, undermined the credibility of the entire casuistical tradition in the ancient and modern world. Hitherto, casuists had thought of virtuous conduct as the pursuit of universal goals. But no matter how attractive the prescriptions of these casuists might be . . . in a post-Humean world they seemed to be arbitrary and dependent on the whims of their authors rather than on a just appreciation of the principles of human nature." Nicholas Phillipson, "Adam Smith as Civic Moralist," in *Wealth and Virtue: The Shaping of Political Economy in the Scottish Enlightenment*, eds. Istvan Hont and Michael Ignatieff (Cambridge: Cambridge University Press, 1983), p. 181. See also Adam Smith, "Of the Manner in Which Different Authors Have Treated the Practical Rules of Morality," in *A Theory of Moral Sentiments* (Indianapolis: Liberty Classics, 1976), pp. 517–37.

21. "Higgling and bargaining" was a favorite phrase of Smith's. See *Wealth of Nations*, I.v.4–6; see also ibid., II.iii.36 and III.iv.1–4.

22. "Smith never discusses systematically when and how we acquire our moral education. He tells us that it is in the family that we first become aware that we are the objects of attention and learn that self-command is a useful habit to acquire in the search for approval, but he only deals in passing with the social experience we undergo thereafter. However, his language is suggestive; outside the family, the capacity for self-command and the rarer capacity for humanity is acquired in 'societies,' 'associations,' 'companies,' 'clubs.' It is the product of the 'ordinary commerce of the world,' in which we seek 'the wise security of friendship' by means of 'conversation' which helps us to acquire ideas of 'independence' and even of 'liberty.'" Phillipson, "Adam Smith" in *Wealth and Virtue*, pp. 187–88.

23. Smith, *Theory of Moral Sentiments*, I.i.5. (pp. 71–72).

24. Alasdair MacIntyre, *Whose Justice? Which Rationality?* (Notre Dame, Ind.: University of Notre Dame Press, 1988), pp. 165–180.

25. David Hume, *Lectures on Jurisprudence. Report of 1762–63.* Quoted by Phillipson, "Adam Smith," in *Wealth and Virtue*, p. 188.

26. Hume, "Of Commerce," *Essays*, pp. 260–61.

27. Ibid., p. 264.

28. Smith, *Wealth of Nations*, p. 418.

29. Smith, *Wealth of Nations*, III.iv.4 (p. 412). See also Hume's argument that the development of commerce had the effect of drawing "authority and consideration to that middling rank of men, who are the best and firmest basis of public liberty." "Of Refinement in the Arts," *Essays*, p. 277.

30. "In the coffee-houses, taverns and salons, men from different walks of life confronted each other as friends and equals and learned that conversation which was the instrument that forged the bonds of friendship. By cultivating the arts of conversation and friendship they would learn to value tolerance, detachment, moderation and a respect for the value of consensus as a means of maintaining the bonds of society." Phillipson, "Adam Smith," in *Wealth and Virtue*, p. 189.

31. "The more [the] refined arts advance," wrote Hume, "the more sociable men become. . . . They flock into cities; love to receive and communicate knowledge; to show their wit or their breeding; their taste in conversation or living, in clothes or furniture. Curiosity allures the wise; vanity the foolish; and pleasure both. Particular clubs and societies are everywhere formed. . . . Thus *industry, knowledge,* and *humanity,* are linked together by an indissoluble chain." "Of Refinement in the Arts," *Essays*, 271. "Before the Seven Years' War . . . the most popular voluntary institution [in Scotland] must have been the sort of club which was modelled on Addison and Steele's Spectator Club. These clubs, which met in the taverns and coffee-houses of countless provincial towns and cities, were small, semi-formal institutions, drawing their members from the ranks of the middling classes of these local communities. Historically, the function of these clubs was to transmit the culture of the metropolis to the provinces, adapting it to local needs and ensuring that it would support and not threaten the sense of identity of increasingly prosperous provincial communities." Phillipson, "Adam Smith," in *Wealth and Virtue*, p. 198.

32. Hume, "Of Commerce," *Essays*, p. 264.

33. Smith, *Wealth of Nations*, IV.iii.c (p. 493).

34. "As far as Smith was concerned, the search for mutual sympathy was a complex and demanding activity. . . . What is curious and distinctive about Smith's theory is that he does not think that we simply put ourselves in another man's shoes in order to see whether, were we him, we would approve of what he was doing. That would have introduced an element of egotism into the theory which he was particularly anxious to avoid. In his account we exercise our imaginative curiosity quite hard in order to achieve what we judge to be a genuinely critical detachment

in our understanding of another man's behaviour." Phillipson, "Adam Smith," in *Wealth and Virtue,* pp. 183–91.

35. Adam Smith and the Scottish social philosophers may be thought of as "practical moralists who had developed a formidable and complex casuistical armoury to instruct young men of middling rank in their duties as men and citizens of a modern commercial polity. Hutcheson, Smith, Ferguson, Reid and Stewart were professors of moral philosophy who saw their curricula as devices to teach their pupils to 'adorn your souls with every virtue, prepare yourselves for every honourable office in life and quench that manly and laudable thirst you should have after knowledge.'" Phillipson, "Adam Smith," in *Wealth and Virtue,* p. 179. For a discussion of Smith's pedagogical method of "presenting his readers (like the audience of fourteen- and fifteen-year-old students who had originally heard his lectures) with a large number of examples to remind them of the pleasure and pain which different types of social encounter could cause," see ibid., pp. 182–83.

36. See Aristotle's discussion of the happiness awaiting the person with a good nature who has been well educated, in *Nichomachean Ethics,* bk. 10, chaps. 6–9 in *The Basic Works of Aristotle,* ed. Richard McKeon (New York: Random House, 1941), pp. 1102–12. On the education of children, see bk. 10, chap. 9 in *Basic Works,* pp. 1108–12.

37. Albert O. Hirschman, *The Passions and the Interests: Political Arguments for Capitalism before Its Triumph* (Princeton: Princeton University Press, 1981).

38. Ibid., p. 32.

39. See Jacob Viner, "Power versus Plenty as Objectives of Foreign Policy in the Seventeenth and Eighteenth Centuries," *World Politics* 1 (1948), reprinted in *Revisions in Mercantilism,* ed. D. C. Coleman (London: Methuen, 1969), pp. 61–91. Cited by Hirschman, *Passions and Interests,* pp. 37–38n.

40. Smith, *Wealth of Nations,* II.iii.28, (pp. 341–42). Emphasis added.

41. Johann Christoph Friedrich von Schiller, *Wallensteins Tod* act 1, sc. 6, line 37. Cited by Hirschman, *Passions and Interests,* p. 48.

42. "I have always considered him," wrote Adam Smith of his friend David Hume, "both in his lifetime and since his death, as approaching as nearly to the idea of a perfectly wise and virtuous man, as perhaps the nature of human frailty will permit." Adam Smith to William Strahan, November 9, 1776, reprinted in Hume, *Essays,* pp. xliv–xlix.

43. Adam Smith was a "practical moralist who thought that his account of the principles of morals and social organization would be of use

to responsibly-minded men of middling rank, living in a modern, commercial society." Phillipson, "Adam Smith," in *Wealth and Virtue*, p. 179.

44. Jules Feiffer, cartoon in *Washington Post*, August 27, 1989.

45. Michael H. Levin, "An Environmental Manifesto for Poland," *Wall Street Journal*, October 24, 1989.

46. See *Sollicitudo Rei Socialis*, no. 15. For the full text and extended commentary, see *Aspiring to Freedom*, ed. Keneth A. Meyers (Grand Rapids, Mich.: Eerdmans, 1988), pp. 16–17.

47. See Hernando de Soto, *The Other Path: The Invisible Revolution in the Third World* (New York: Harper and Row, 1989).

FOUR   CAMELS AND NEEDLES, TALENTS AND TREASURE:
        AMERICAN CATHOLICISM AND THE CAPITALIST ETHIC

1. See, for example, the Carrolls' correspondence with George Washington on the latter's inauguration as first president under the Constitution of 1787, in *Documents of American Catholic History*, ed. John Tracy Ellis (Wilmington: Michael Glazier, 1987), 1: 169–72.

2. On spirituality in Catholic Maryland, see Jay Dolan, *The American Catholic Experience* (New York: Doubleday, 1985), pp. 80–97; Joseph P. Chinnici, O.F.M., *Living Stones: The History and Structure of Catholic Spiritual Life in the United States* (New York: Macmillan, 1989), pp. 26–34.

3. See Richard Shaw, *Dagger John: The Unquiet Life and Times of Archbishop John Hughes of New York* (New York: Paulist Press, 1977), for an extended portrait of this remarkable figure.

4. John Hughes, "A Lecture on the Importance of a Christian Basis for the Science of Political Economy, and Its Application to the Affairs of Life," in *American Catholic Religious Thought*, ed. Patrick W. Carey (New York: Paulist Press, 1987), pp. 202–203. Hughes's lecture was delivered to the Calvert Institute in Baltimore and the Carroll Institute in Philadelphia on January 17 and 18, 1844.

5. Orestes Brownson, "The Laboring Class," *Boston Quarterly Review* 3, quoted in John J. Mitchell, *Critical Voices in American Catholic Economic Thought* (New York: Paulist Press, 1989), p. 8.

6. Ibid., p. 20.

7. Ibid.

8. Ibid., p. 9.

9. See Mitchell, *Critical Voices*, p. 18.

10. Ibid., p. 19.

11. Ibid.

12. For a succinct summary of the McGlynn Affair, see Gerald Fogarty, S.J., *The Vatican and the American Hierarchy from 1870 to 1965* (Wilmington: Michael Glazier, 1985), pp. 93–114.

13. See Marvin R. O'Connell, *John Ireland and the American Catholic Church* (St. Paul: Minnesota Historical Society, 1988), pp. 378ff.

14. Details may be found in Fogarty, *The Vatican and the American Hierarchy*, pp. 87–92.

15. Ibid., p. 91.

16. Quoted in ibid., p. 238.

17. Ibid., p. 237. For a more complete analysis of the Bishops' Program, see Joseph M. McShane, S.J., *"Sufficiently Radical": Catholicism, Progressivism, and the Bishops' Program of 1919* (Washington: Catholic University of America Press, 1986).

18. McShane, *Sufficiently Radical*, p. 199.

19. Quoted in Fogarty, *The Vatican and the American Hierarchy*, p. 238.

20. Dennis McCann, "Option for the Poor: Rethinking a Catholic Tradition," in *The Preferential Option for the Poor*, ed. Richard J. Neuhaus (Grand Rapids, Mich.: Eerdmans, 1988), p. 51.

21. The most prominent example of this kind of analysis is Michael Novak, *The Spirit of Democratic Capitalism* (New York: Simon and Schuster, 1982).

22. See *Gaudium et Spes*, pp. 63–72.

23. For an analysis of *Populorum Progressio*, see my *Catholicism and the Renewal of American Democracy* (New York: Paulist Press, 1989), pp. 174–78.

24. For an overview of the liberation theology agenda and its impact on American Catholic thinking, see my *Tranquillitas Ordinis: The Present Failure and Future Promise of American Catholic Thought on War and Peace* (New York: Oxford University Press, 1987), pp. 286–300. See also Michael Novak, *Will It Liberate? Questions for Liberation Theology* (New York: Paulist Press, 1987).

25. For a sympathetic analysis of Maurin's and Day's positions, and their roots in Maurin's Christian personalism (itself influenced by the French moral theologian Emmanuel Mounier), see William D. Miller, *A Harsh and Dreadful Love: Dorothy Day and the Catholic Worker Movement* (New York: Liveright, 1973).

26. See Andrew M. Greeley, *The American Catholic: A Social Portrait* (New York: Basic Books, 1977).

27. Michael Novak has, again, been in the forefront of this discussion. See *Spirit of Democratic Capitalism,* chap. 20; *Toward a Theology of the Corporation* (Washington: American Enterprise Institute, 1981); *The American Vision: An Essay on the Future of Democratic Capitalism* (Washington: American Enterprise Institute, 1981).

28. For an overview of the theory of the new class, see Peter L. Berger, "Ethics and the Present Class Struggle," *Worldview* (April 1978): 6–11.

29. For an account of some of the dominant currents of thought in the American Catholic new class, see my *Catholicism and the Renewal of American Democracy,* chap. 3.

30. This motivation has been hotly denied by those responsible for the official hermeneutics of "Economic Justice for All," but I first heard it in personal conversation from Bishop Rosazza himself, who presumably knows what he, at least, was up to.

31. On this point, see Jim Castelli, *The Bishops and the Bomb: Waging Peace in a Nuclear Age* (Garden City: Doubleday Image Books, 1983), p. 15. Since Castelli's is a semiofficial history of the 1983 pastoral, his judgment on this point, at least, is virtually unassailable.

32. "Economic Justice for All," nos. 30–55.

33. Ibid., no. 98.

34. Ibid., no. 117.

35. John Langan, S.J., "Afterword: A Direction for the Future," in *The Catholic Challenge to the American Economy: Reflections on the U.S. Bishops' Pastoral Letter on Catholic Social Teaching and the U.S. Economy,* ed. Thomas M. Gannon, S.J. (New York: Macmillan, 1987), p. 264.

36. Some—Ernest van den Haag comes to mind—might argue that this missed opportunity in American Catholicism is primarily due to what is taken to be Rome's continued nervousness about, bordering on animus against, capitalism. Wrote van den Haag recently, "The Roman Catholic Church . . . has always been allergic to economic reasoning. The love for the poor, the failures, the simpletons, the oppressed, and the degraded, which the Gospels so magnificently commend, has often turned into a love for poverty and failure, and—more important—into a hostility to success and wealth, and to a system that permits either. Yet the Gospels merely assign a low priority to worldly success. They are not hostile to it. Renunciation of the world is favored for the sake of one's soul. But merely being poor without having renounced anything is no virtue, any more than being rich without having deprived anybody is a vice. Helping is meritorious. Needing help is not." Ernest van den Haag, "The War Between Paleos and Neos," *National Review* (February 24, 1989): 23.

William McGurn's essay, "Preferential Option: Why Manila Is Poor and Hong Kong Is Rich," *Crisis* (June 1989): 27–32, argues that classic Roman economic thought suffers from "fundamentally materialist assumptions about economic life," and takes "an essentially managerial approach to wealth that ignores the infusion of human faith and creativity that brings it into being."

However one assesses the impact of the Roman magisterium's "allergy" to capitalism on the failure to develop an ethic and spirituality of wealth creation in American Catholicism—and I am inclined to think that the least one can say is that the magisterium failed to encourage such a development—Rome seems an unlikely place to locate the ideological roots of the American Catholic new class's opposition to an ethic of wealth creation, for it is precisely against Rome that much of the current American Catholic intellectual and opinion establishment defines itself. Father Richard McBrien, for example, may find it titillating to cite *Sollicitudo Rei Socialis* in his polemics against Michael Neuhaus, Richard Neuhaus, and the author of this paper (see McBrien's column, "Encyclical Poses Complex Challenges," *Brooklyn Tablet* [April 16, 1988]); but no one who has followed McBrien's writing carefully will think that he takes his economics, any more than he takes his moral theology, his ecclesiology, or his understanding of church-state relations, from Karol Wojtyla and Joseph Ratzinger.

The roots of the American Catholic new class's animus against capitalism lie in a variety of vulgarized Marxist themes, which are given a patina of respectability through the selective citation of Roman documents. In school, we used to call that eisegesis.

37. See Gregory Baum, *The Priority of Labor: A Commentary on "Laborem Exercens"* (New York: Paulist Press, 1982).

38. See, for example, John Gray, "The Last Socialist?" *National Review* (June 30, 1989): 27–29, 31.

39. *Sollicitudo Rei Socialis,* p. 15.

40. *Laborem Exercens,* p. 25.

41. The biblical warrant for this identification may be found in the parable of the talents (Matt. 25:14–30).

42. Lay Commission on Catholic Social Thought and the U.S. Economy, "Toward the Future: A Lay Letter," p. 28.

43. See, for example, *Sollicitudo Rei Socialis,* p. 42; "Economic Justice for All," p. 87.

44. McCann, "Option for the Poor," in *Preferential Option,* pp. 37–44.

45. Ibid., p. 44.

46. Peter L. Berger, *The Capitalist Revolution* (New York: Basic Books, 1986).

47. Ralph McInerny, "Maritain in and on America," in *Reinhold Niebuhr Today,* ed. Richard John Neuhaus (Grand Rapids, Mich.: Eerdmans, 1989), p. 37.

48. Jacques Maritain, *Reflections on America* (New York: Charles Scribner's Sons, 1958), pp. 30, 33, 35.

49. Josef Pieper, *Leisure: The Basis of Culture* (New York: New American Library, 1963).

50. *Laborem Exercens,* preface.

51. Ibid., p. 25.

52. Gilbert Meilaender, "To Throw Oneself into the Wave: The Problem of Possessions," in *Preferential Option,* pp. 79–80.

53. Ibid., p. 80.

54. Ibid.

55. Ibid., p. 81.

FIVE   PRIVATE PROPERTY, ETHICS, AND WEALTH CREATION

1. The case against wealth distribution is far stronger, from a moral perspective, since it is impossible to distinguish this activity from theft. See my treatment, later in this chapter, of the biblical commandment against stealing.

2. The best known modern-day scholars associated with this perspective are Milton Friedman, Friedrich Hayek, Murray Rothbard, James Buchanan, George Stigler, Richard Epstein, David Friedman, Walter Williams, Henry Hazlitt, and Robert Nozick (at least in his *Anarchy, State, and Utopia* [New York: Basic Books, 1974], if not in his later writings). In the recent past, such writers as Ludwig von Mises, Albert Jay Nock, John T. Flynn, Frank Chodorov, Felix Morley, H. L. Mencken, Lysander Spooner, and Benjamin R. Tucker would have to be included under this rubric.

3. From a religious point of view we are, of course, not self-owners. Rather, God created us, and we are therefore owned by Him. Insofar as strictly interpersonal relations are concerned, however—those which obtain strictly between one human being and another—the basic axiom of nonagression against nonagressors can still be maintained; and thus our ownership by God is entirely consistent with the philosophy of libertarianism. Although between a human and his or her Higher Power the appropriate relation may be one of slave to master, or steward to

owner, this does not at all hold true between one human and another. That is to say, we are each stewards of our own bodies, answerable only to God for how we treat them; no power on this earth—religious or secular—has the right to interfere with how we treat ourselves, for to do so would be to trespass on the relation between human beings and God.

4. Milton Friedman, *There's No Such Thing as a Free Lunch* (La Salle, Ill.: Open Court Publishing Co., 1975), chap. 8; Friedman, *The Essence of Friedman* (Stanford, Calif.: Hoover Institution Press, 1987), chap. 7.

5. Other perspectives, to be sure, would agree with the nonaggression axiom. Even public opinion is overwhelmingly in support of such a view. The distinctiveness of libertarianism is not that it, too, upholds the axiom, but that it makes it a basic premise of its entire system, and rigorously adheres to it. See in this regard Murray N. Rothbard, *For a New Liberty* (New York: Macmillan, 1973); and *The Ethics of Liberty* (Atlantic Highlands, N.J.: Humanities Press, 1982).

6. Being a member of the Aryan race, or having red hair, or being able to run a mile in less than four minutes, are certainly characteristics that distinguish those to whom they apply from most other people; but they are not morally relevant, and thus cannot be used to justify the rule of one over another.

7. Hans-Hermann Hoppe, *A Theory of Socialism and Capitalism* (Boston: Kluwer, 1989).

8. Rothbard, *The Ethics of Liberty;* Nozick, *Anarchy, State, and Utopia;* Richard Epstein, *Takings: Private Property and the Power of Eminent Domain* (Cambridge: Harvard University Press, 1985); and Bernard H. Siegan, *Economic Liberties and the Constitution* (Chicago: University of Chicago Press, 1980).

9. What of the objection that there can be no justification for private property rights because property itself is intrinsically an illegitimate institution? This sentiment is often buttressed by citing Proudhon, who is widely quoted as having held that "Property is theft." There is something logically incongruous about this statement, however. "Property is theft" is used to denigrate the ownership of property; but in fact the very concept of "theft" makes no sense in the absence of legitimate property. If there were no legitimately owned private property, there logically could be no such thing as theft. Consider an act that might otherwise be considered to be stealing. Without a perspective of property rights, if someone were to take an object out of the possession of another person, and place it into his or her own possession, we could not call this theft, and by implication label it as illegitimate. Rather, we would have to

unsatisfactorily (and amorally) describe it as "transferring," or "conveying," or "relocating." To do so would be to eviscerate the ordinary meaning of the word.

10. For a full explication of this statement, see Nozick, *Anarchy, State, and Utopia* for adumbration of the legitimate process of property acquisition.

11. John Locke, "An Essay Concerning the True Original Extent and End of Civil Government," in *Social Contract*, ed. E. Barker (New York: Oxford University Press, 1948), p.8. Homesteading theory has been subjected to a thoroughgoing critique by Nozick, in *Anarchy, State, and Utopia*. For a defense against this attack, see Jeffrey Paul, ed., *On Reading Nozick* (New York: Rowan and Littlefield, 1983).

12. There are those who will claim that the government represents us all, especially when democracy is the political system utilized. For a critique of this view, see Lysander Spooner, *No Treason* (Larkspur, Colo., 1966. First published in 1870). More basic, however, is the issue of why the entire populace, whether through the intermediation of the state or not, is entitled to land to which they have done nothing. Moreover, if the citizenry of one nation can own land that they have not earned in any meaningful manner, this applies logically to the world as a whole. Specifically, it would justify the Law of the Sea treaty, which claims that all the people of the earth equally own the ocean's resources. This same line of reasoning could be applied to the moon and the neighboring planets. These are, however, the precise principles that underlie Soviet agriculture. It would be difficult to imagine a recipe better designed to bring about economic stagnation with regard to the exploration and exploitation of the seas and the heavenly bodies.

13. One also engages in a performative contradiction when one asserts that it is improper to own physical property. One must necessarily use property in order to make any such assertion (floor space, etc.); and in doing so, if one is to act legitimately, one must either own the property in question, or obtain the owner's permission to do so. In either case, private property rights are also presupposed. See Hoppe, "On Praxeology and the Praxeological Foundations of Epistemology and Ethics" (1987). Mimeo.

14. Those theologians who are looking for a "third way" that is confined neither to socialism nor to capitalism could thus do worse than consider libertarianism.

15. The egalitarian ideal is far from achieved in places like Cuba, the Soviet Union, the People's Republic of China, Eastern Europe, and the

Marxist dictatorships in Africa. For a critique of coercive socialism, see Ludwig Mises, *Socialism* (Indianapolis: Liberty Fund, 1981. First published in 1969); Friedrich A. Hayek, *The Road to Serfdom* (Chicago: University of Chicago Press, 1944); Hayek, ed., *Capitalism and the Historians,* essays by T. S. Ashton, L. M. Hacker, W. H. Hutt, and B. de Jouvenel (Chicago: University of Chicago Press, 1954); and Hayek, *The Fatal Conceit: The Errors of Socialism* (Chicago: University of Chicago Press, 1989).

16. In fact, unfortunately, kibbutzim in Israel are heavily subsidized by the state through coercive taxation; but this does not destroy the ideal of the kibbutz, run on strictly voluntary principles. Such a union would have to disavow all initiations of force, whether de facto or de jure. It would have to limit itself to organizing mass quits, or threats thereof, when working conditions were not to its liking. It could not interfere with the right of the employer and alternative workers (e.g., strikebreakers, "scabs") to bargain with each other and to ignore the union. It is an unhappy fact that there are no such entities in existence at present; but this does not negate the possibility of such an institution. At least with regard to the adult members, who, in any case, are the only ones to whom the concept of voluntary acts could fully apply.

17. Other instances of voluntary socialism are the mediating institutions, such as churches, charitable organizations, and service, social, religious, and sports clubs, which stand between the individual and the society at large. See John W. Cooper, *The Theology of Freedom* (Macon, Ga.: Mercer University Press, 1985), pp. 100–107, 125–31; Robert Benne, *The Ethic of Democratic Capitalism* (Philadelphia: Fortress Press, 1981); and Michael Novak, *The Spirit of Democratic Capitalism* (New York: Simon and Schuster, 1982).

18. There are those who misinterpret libertarianism as opposing voluntary or mediating institutions. They criticize this philosophy as excessively individualistic, as one which somehow compels the individual to take on atomistic relationships, ignoring all other people, except perhaps for commercial interactions. In their view, the philosophy of voluntarism eschews all relationships other than the commercial; it has a cash register instead of a heart; it denigrates the relationships of friendship, and all other humanistic impulses as well. The present analysis of voluntary socialism is one attempt to put this canard to rest. See also the contributions to George W. Carey, ed., *Freedom and Virtue* (Lanham, Md.: University Press of America, 1984) by Robert Nisbet, Walter Berns, and especially Russell Kirk.

Michael Novak, in "Boredom, Virtue and Democratic Capitalism," *Commentary* (September 1989) 88, no. 3, p. 34, deflects a similar charge made against the neoconservative perspective of democratic capitalism, but his words could serve as well for the libertarian defense against the criticism of atomism:

> Such a judgment springs from what logicians call a category mistake—and a horrific one. A democratic capitalist regime is not the kingdom of God. It is not a church, or even a philosophy, and it is only in an outward sense "a way of life." . . . The construction of a social order that achieves these is *not* designed to fill the soul, or to teach a philosophy, or to give instruction in how to live. It is designed to create *space,* within which the soul may make its own choices, and within which spiritual leaders and spiritual associations may do their own necessary and creative work.

And so it is for the libertarian philosophy. It, too, is not a religion, nor a recipe for living properly, nor a way of life. It, too, is designed to create space for individuals; it sets up appropriate boundaries around each person, and labels as invasive and unjust all uninvited crossings of these boundaries.

It cannot be overly emphasized that libertarianism, in confining itself to issues concerning the use of force, is an extremely limited ideology. It does not contemplate many important issues. But just as specialization and the division of labor are important concepts in economics, so are they in all intellectual and ethical pursuits.

19. The market is set up so as to satisfy the consumer. Sometimes, however, the consumer demands products that are properly considered immoral; examples such as pornography, prostitution, and certain drugs come to mind. It would be improper to blame the free enterprise system for this occurrence. Presumably, a voluntarily socialist system could produce these goods and services, were its members interested in them. The libertarian view on this phenomenon is thus not that the market (or economic freedom) always precludes the production of items of questionable morality, but only that the production and sale of these items should not be made an indictable offense, because it does not necessarily involve the initiation of violence. See E. J. Mishan, "Religion, Culture and Technology," in *The Morality of the Market: Religious and Economic Perspectives,* ed. Walter Block, Geoffrey Brennan, and Kenneth Elzinga (Vancouver: Fraser Institute, 1985).

20. True, I may have been in a bad state beforehand. This is indicated, perhaps, by the fact that my position is improved through employment at $5 per hour. But this is not necessarily the fault of my new employer! Assume that it is not. Assume, that is, that my unfortunate preemployment condition was due to some other cause. Then it is clear that my employer is my benefactor, even if my position is a very humble one.

21. Consider a possible objection. When Henry Ford began mass-producing the "horseless carriage," he undoubtedly benefited millions of people. For the first time in the history of the world, this item became more than a plaything for the rich: the middle class, and then even the poor, were able to own automobiles. But what about the capitalists and workers in the horse and buggy industry: the horsebreakers and trainers, the carriage, bridle, and buggy whip manufacturers, the skilled artisans who created saddles? Weren't they hurt by the free market? The answer is, no. The market consists solely of the voluntary trades that actually take place. After the advent of Ford, virtually no one was willing to trade anything for the particular skills of the members of the horse and buggy industry. By definition, they were no longer part of the market (although, to be sure, before the automobile they were an integral part of the market). After the introduction of the car, these people had a choice: to remain outside the market and not benefit from it, or to orient themselves to the market and begin supplying things that the consumers now wanted to purchase. The market benefits all participants, but not everyone necessarily chooses to be a participant.

22. When this occurs in the third world, it is particularly vicious. There are numerous cases on record where the indigenous peoples were relatively happy in their pre–(coercive)capitalist tribal life, or at least unwilling to work for a multinational enterprise (MNE) for money wages. The local government, at the behest of the MNE, then began taxing the natives and forced them to pay in the form of money, not goods—and money was only available from the (coercive) capitalist. In this way the MNE could in effect enslave the natives (that is, force unwilling persons to become employees). See Parker T. Moon, *Imperialism and World Politics* (New York: Diamond, 1927).

These, however, are coercive MNEs. If our analysis is to be coherent and rational, they must be sharply distinguished from voluntary multinational corporations, which since they are part of the mutually beneficial free enterprise system, can only benefit all those with whom they come in contact. See Peter T. Bauer, *Equality, the Third World, and Economic Delusion* (Cambridge: Harvard University Press, 1981); Michael Novak, ed., *The Denigration of Capitalism* (Washington, D.C.: American Enterprise Institute for Public Policy Research, 1979); and Novak, ed., *The Corporation: A Theological Inquiry* (Washington, D.C.: American Enterprise Institute for Public Policy Research, 1981).

23. Nozick, *Anarchy, State, and Utopia.*

24. It is often claimed that cooperation takes place under socialism, and competition under capitalism. Limiting our vision to only the voluntary versions of both these systems, we can see that there is a grain of truth in this assertion. That is, explicit cooperation takes place only in voluntary socialism, not voluntary capitalism. However, implicit cooperation takes place in the latter system; for example, in the market, if everyone wanted to be a carpenter, and no one a plumber, the wages of carpenters would fall calamitously and those of plumbers would rise sharply. This would induce at least some people to give up a life of carpentering and embrace one of plumbing. If the allocation between these two callings still did not match the relative desires of consumers for their services, there would yet remain a wage gap, inducing further changes. It takes no great insight to see that the market system is really enticing people into cooperating with each other in this regard. As Adam Smith said, each person is only attempting to further his own private interest, but in so doing he is led, as if by an invisible hand, to benefit the public—which was no part of his intention. Theologians see the hand of God in every part of our existence, even in the most unlikely of places: in a sunset, in music, in mathematics, in a baby's smile. Why is it that there is very little appreciation that the free market, too, is part of God's plan, and so is the invisible hand identified by Adam Smith? For further elucidation and elaboration, see Walter Block, *The U.S. Bishops and Their Critics: An Economic and Ethical Perspective* (Vancouver: Fraser Institute, 1986); and Michael Novak, *Capitalism and Socialism* (Washington, D.C.: American Enterprise Institute for Public Policy Research, 1979).

25. Irving Kristol, *Two Cheers for Capitalism* (New York: Basic Books, 1978), p. xii, for example, says: "The welfare state . . . need be no threat, in principle, to capitalism. An affluent society in which people choose to purchase (through taxes) certain goods collectively rather than individually . . . represents no rebellion against the liberal capitalist order." For other neoconservative writing that advocates the welfare state, see Melville J. Ulmer, *The Welfare State* (Boston: Houghton Mifflin, 1969), p. 170; Michael Novak, "The Liberal Society as Liberation Theology," *Notre Dame Journal of Law, Ethics and Public Policy* (1985), 2, no. 1:

31; Benne, *The Ethic of Democratic Capitalism,* p. 79; and Daniel Bell, *The Cultural Contradictions of Capitalism* (New York: Basic Books, 1976), p. 226.

One difficulty with this line of reasoning is that if the capitalist order is based on anything, it is based on the sanctity of private property rights. These cannot be reconciled with a system under which they may be violated provided only that a majority of the voters agree. Democratic capitalism is not an unlimited system, wherein the citizens can vote on whatever they please. On the contrary, it is a constitutional democracy bound by a certain set of rules and principles; foremost among them is the inviolability of persons and their private property. If mere majority vote could justify any outcome, our moral analysis of the Nazi epoch would have to be fundamentally altered.

Another problem is that the welfare state is an example of coercive collectivism, not the voluntary variety. The minority, which is forced to relinquish money to the state for welfare programs against its will, cannot be said to have agreed to it. Had welfare been brought in by referendum, then at least an argument along these lines could be attempted; but it was not. It might be argued that although the minority did not agree to the specific vote that indirectly led to the welfare state, it agreed to the process whereby such courses of action could be chosen, and therefore the ultimate decision was a voluntary one. However, the recipients of governmental subsidies are almost always more highly concentrated than are the taxpayers who must foot the bill. Milton Friedman, *Capitalism and Freedom* (Chicago: University of Chicago Press, 1962), p. 143. Indeed, the average citizen engages in "rational ignorance" of the political process, since his or her one vote has so little effect. Under these conditions, it is difficult to regard political outcomes as voluntary in the same way as, for example, decisions to engage in market activity. It is entirely conceivable that a majority could oppose a welfare system, and yet it might arise out of the representational political system; see James M. Buchanan and Gordon Tullock, *The Calculus of Consent: Logical Foundations of Constitutional Democracy* (Ann Arbor: University of Michigan, 1971). See also Spooner, *No Treason,* on the fallacy of regarding the outcomes of political and economic activity as equally voluntary.

William E. Simon, "Non-Zoning in Houston," *Journal of Law and Economics* (April 1978), 13, no. 1, pp. 225–27, characterizes such neoconservative defenders of the welfare state as Kristol, Wilson, Glazer, Bell, Novak and Hook as "scholars of a New Deal stripe," and criticizes them as "interventionists to a degree that I myself do not endorse." See also Friedrich A. Hayek, "Why I Am Not a Conservative," in *The Constitution of Liberty* (Chicago: Henry Regnery Co., 1960); and Milton and Rose Friedman, *Free to Choose* (New York: Avon Books, 1981), who sharply criticize the New Deal in a chapter entitled "From Cradle to Grave."

26. George Gilder, *Wealth and Poverty* (New York: Basic Books, 1981), p. 122, says: "Welfare, by far the largest economic influence in the ghetto, exerts a constant, seductive, erosive pressure on the marriages and work habits of the poor, and over the years, in poor communities, it fosters a durable 'welfare culture.' . . . Welfare continuously mutes and misrepresents the necessities of life that prompted previous generations of poor people to escape poverty through the invariable routes of work, family and faith."

27. Unfortunately, there are numerous moralistic and ecclesiastical criticisms of the markets, free enterprise, and the flexible price system. These criticisms have the effect of immiserating the poor—the very opposite of their intentions. For a recent and highly publicized example, see U.S. Bishops, "Pastoral Letter on Catholic Social Teaching and the U.S. Economy: Origins," *NC Documentary Service* (November 15, 1984), 14, no. 22/23. For a neoconservative critique of this document, see Michael Novak, et al., *Toward the Future: Catholic Social Thought and the U.S. Economy—A Lay Letter* (New York: Lay Commission on Catholic Social Teaching and the U.S. Economy, 1984); Novak, "The Two Catholic Letters on the U.S. Economy," in *Challenge and Response,* ed. Robert Royal (Washington, D.C.: Ethics and Public Policy Center, 1985), pp. 30–32; Novak, "The Liberal Society as Liberation Theology"; and Paul Heyne, *The U.S. Catholic Bishops and the Pursuit of Justice* (Washington, D.C.: Cato Institute, 1985), Cato Policy Analysis no. 50. For a critique of these documents from a libertarian perspective, see Block, *The U.S. Bishops and Their Critics: An Economic and Ethical Perspective.* See also Ronald H. Nash, *Poverty and Wealth* (Westchester, Ill.: Crossway Books, 1986); Nash, "The Two Faces of Evangelical Concern," in *Piety and Politics,* ed. Richard J. Neuhaus and Michael Cromartie (Lanham, Md.: University Press of America, 1987); Alejandro Chafuen, *Christians for Freedom* (San Francisco: Ignatius Press, 1986); Walter E. Williams, "Good Intentions—Bad Results: The Economic Pastoral and America's Disadvantaged," *Notre Dame Journal of Law, Ethics and Public Policy,* 2, no. 1 (1985); Richard A. Posner, "Wealth Maximization Revisited," *Notre Dame Journal of Law, Ethics and Public Policy,* 2, no. 1

(1985); Bauer, "Ecclesiastical Economics Is Envy Exalted," *This World* (Winter/Spring 1982), no. 1; James V. Schall, S.J., *Religion, Wealth and Poverty* (Vancouver: Fraser Institute, 1989); Doug Bandow, *Beyond Good Intentions* (Westchester, Ill.: Crossway Books, 1988); and James A. Sadowsky, S.J., "Capitalism, Ethics and Classical Catholic Social Doctrine," *This World* (Fall 1983), no. 6. Reprinted as "Classical Social Doctrine in the Roman Catholic Church," *Religion, Economics and Social Thought,* eds. Walter Block and Irving Hexham (Vancouver: Fraser Institute, 1986).

28. Friedman and Friedman, *Tyranny of the Status Quo* (San Diego: Harcourt Brace Jovanovich, 1983).

29. There is a wide consensus among economists that such policies are undesirable. See Bruno S. Frey, Werner W. Pommerehne, Friedrich Schneider, and Guy Gilbert, "Consensus and Dissension among Economists: An Empirical Inquiry," *American Economic Review* (December 1984), 74, no. 5, pp. 986–94; and Michael A. Walker and Walter Block, "Entropy in the Canadian Economics Profession: Sampling Consensus on the Major Issues," *Canadian Public Policy* (June 1988), 14, no. 2.

30. The case for privatization of government property is the libertarian answer to the conundrum raised by Richard John Neuhaus, *The Naked Public Square: Religion and Democracy in America* (New York: Eerdmans, 1982). Privatize the public square to the greatest extent possible, consistent with the limited-government philosophy, and the question of whether and to what degree religious discourse may take place on public property tends to disappear.

Williams, *The State against Blacks;* Thomas Borcherding, *The Egg Marketing Board* (Vancouver: Fraser Institute, 1981); Herbert G. Grubel and Richard W. Schwindt, *The Real Cost of the B.C. Milk Board* (Vancouver: Fraser Institute, 1977); T. M. Ohashi, T. P. Roth, Z. A. Spindler, M. L. McMillan, and K. H. Norrie, *Privation Theory and Practice* (Vancouver: Fraser Institute, 1980); Richard B. McKenzie, *Fugitive Industry: The Economics and Politics of Deindustrialization* (Cambridge, Mass.: Ballinger Publishing Co., 1984); Siegan, "Non-Zoning in Houston," *Journal of Law and Economics* (April 1970), 13, no. 1; Henry Hazlitt, *Economics in One Lesson* (New York: Arlington House Publishers, 1979); Herbert G. Grubel and Michael A. Walker, eds., *Unemployment Insurance: Global Evidence of Its Effects on Unemployment* (Vancouver: Fraser Institute, 1976); Dominick T. Armentano, *The Myths of Antitrust* (New Rochelle, N.Y.: Arlington House, 1972); Armentano, *Antitrust and Monopoly: Anatomy of a Policy Failure* (New York: Wiley,

1982); Henry A. Manne, *Insider Trading and the Stock Market* (New York: Free Press, 1966); Manne, "In Defense of Insider Trading," *Harvard Business Review* (November/December 1966), 113; Murray Rothbard, *Power and Market: Government and the Economy* (Menlo Park, Calif.: Institute for Humane Studies, 1970), pp. 30–41; Friedman and Friedman, *Free to Choose*, pp. 27–28; and Friedman, *Capitalism and Freedom*.

31. However, there are some neoconservatives who specifically call for regulation of the economy. Michael Novak ("The Two Catholic Letters on the U.S. Economy," p. 31) states: "Such steps do not *contradict* a successful capitalist economy; on the contrary, they are indispensable to it. Similarly, a free market economy *requires* regulation and cannot function without it." It is difficult to understand the assertion that economic freedom requires regulation of the economy. See Michael A. Walker, *Freedom, Democracy and Economic Welfare* (Vancouver: Fraser Institute, 1988) in this regard.

32. Friedman, "Alleviation of Poverty," in *The Economics of Poverty: An American Paradox*, ed. Burton A. Weisbrod (Englewood Cliffs, N.J.: Prentice-Hall, 1965), p. 151 states: "One recourse (to poverty), and in many ways the most desirable, is private charity. It is noteworthy that the heyday of laissez-faire, the middle and late 19th century, in Britain and the U.S., saw an extraordinary proliferation of private eleemosynary organizations and institutions. One of the major costs of the extension of governmental welfare activities has been the corresponding decline in private charitable activities."

33. Walter E. Williams, "They Want Something in Return," *Conservative Chronicle* (July 1989) states:

Charity is one of man's noblest virtues. With America doing about 85% of all world giving, we can rightfully be pround of ourselves. "Public charity" is a sin which trashes both the concept and spirit of true charity. After all, charity is a voluntary act of conscience, but what Congress gives away is obtained through threats, intimidation and coercion.

To my knowledge, only one congressman saw government largess for what it is. Rep. David Crockett, Democrat from Tennessee who later died defending the Alamo, challenged Congress' wish to assist the widow of a distinguished naval officer. Crockett said, "We have the right, as individuals, to give away as much or our own money as we please in charity. . . . We have not the semblance of authority to appropriate it [taxpayers' money] as charity." He realized that giving away taxpayers' money was closer to theft than charity.

34. When a group such as the New York City chapter of the American Society for the Prevention of Cruelty to Animals decides to kill cats and dogs rather than give them to people who work during normal business hours, donors can easily divert funds to more commonsensical organizations. This power of the purse will likely convince the ASPCA to reconsider its policy. Were this organization in the public sector, it would be far less responsive to the desires of contributors.

35. Arnold Brown, "The Shadow Side of Affluence: The Welfare System and the Welfare of the Needy," *Fraser Forum* (October 1987).

36. Thomas Sowell, *The Economics and Politics of Race: An International Perspective* (New York: Morrow, 1983).

37. The infamous Housing and Urban Development scandal is but the latest in a long train of abuses illustrating the fact that money ostensibly earmarked for the poor by the welfare state does not always end up in their hands. Nor is this an aberration. Williams, in "They Want Something in Return," states, with regard to political scandals:

> Why would people, legally or illegally, give money and favors to members of Congress in the first place? The answer is simple; they expect to get something in return. So long as we permit our lawmakers to use their positions to give certain Americans money earned by other Americans and grant special privileges, no matter how much we strengthen ethics rules, we are going to have corruption of public officials. The only change we can expect is greater efforts to avoid the appearance of wrongdoing.

38. Dwight Lee, "The Politics of Poverty and the Poverty of Politics," *Cato Journal* (Spring 1985), 5, no. 1, p. 20. This public-choice perspective makes it easier to understand the HUD scandal as an example of business as usual, and not as an anomaly. For an alternative explanation of the functioning of the welfare state, see Frances Fox Piven and Richard A. Cloward, *Regulating the Poor: The Functions of Public Welfare* (New York: Random House, 1971).

39. Charles Murray, *Losing Ground: American Social Policy from 1950 to 1980* (New York: Basic Books, 1984).

40. Numerous commentators cite Sweden as a counterexample to this contention, and claim that the experience of that country shows that

massive income redistribution need not have strong disincentive effects. However, the Swedish welfare state did not really expand to its present preeminence until the late 1960s. At that time, Sweden had one of the highest per capita incomes in the world; but this cannot be attributed to coercive socialism, since the economy was relatively free in the preceding century, during which Sweden's growth rate was among the highest in the world, second only to Japan's. However, according to the findings of Assar Lindbeck, "Swedish Industry in a National and an International Perspective," *Skandinaviska Enskilds Bankan Quarterly Review* (1988), no. 3, Swedish economic growth from 1970 to 1985, the period when the economic effects of the heavy redistributionist policies took effect, was only 1.1 percent annually. This was the lowest of all the Organization for Economic Cooperation and Development countries, even including pre-Thatcher Great Britain. As a result of this poor economic performance, Sweden now ranks nineteenth in terms of real disposable household income, below such countries as Spain, Italy, and Ireland.

41. Gilder, *Wealth and Poverty.*

42. William Tucker, "Black Family Agonistes," *American Spectator* (July 1984), pp. 14–17.

43. Friedman, "Alleviation of Poverty," pp. 151, 152.

44. Epstein, *Takings: Private Property and the Power of Eminent Domain*, p. 317. See also Walter Block, "Public Goods and Externalities: The Case of Roads," *Journal of Libertarian Studies* 7, no.1 (Spring 1983); and Jeffrey Hummel, "National Goods vs. Public Goods: Defense, Disarmament and Free Riders," *Review of Austrian Economics* 4 (1990).

45. Peter T. Bauer, *Reality and Rhetoric: Studies in the Economics of Development* (Cambridge: Harvard University Press, 1984); see also Friedman, *The Essence of Friedman.*

46. Bauer, *Reality and Rhetoric;* see also Basil S. Yamey, *The Economics of Underdeveloped Countries* (Chicago: University of Chicago Press, 1957); Bauer, *Equality, the Third World, and Economic Delusion;* Michael Novak, *Will It Liberate?* (New York: Paulist Press, 1986); and Novak, *Liberation South, Liberation North* (Washington, D.C.: American Enterprise Institute for Public Policy Research, 1981).

47. Bauer, "Ecclesiastical Economics: Envy Exalted" in *Reality and Rhetoric.*

48. Stephen Cox, Mike Molmes, R. W. Bradford, and Timothy Virkkala, "Survey: The Liberty Poll," *Liberty* (July 1988), 1, no. 6, p. 47, report that only 23 percent of the sample in their survey of libertarians had any religious affiliation at all.

49. Cox et al., "Survey: The Liberty Poll," p. 41.

50. Examples of such people include, in addition to the present author, Doug Bandow; Alejandro Chafuen; James Fisher, C.S.P.; Marshall Fritz; P. J. Hill; Leonard Liggio; Ron Paul; Joseph Peden; Murray Rothbard; James Sadowsky, S.J.; Lee Shubert (editor of *Gallatians Seven: A Christian Libertarian Newsletter*); Robert Sirico, C.S.P.; and Jeffrey Tucker.

51. Cox et al., "Survey: The Liberty Poll," p. 41.

52. Murray Rothbard, "Freedom Is for Everyone," *Liberty* (March 1988), 1, no. 4, p. 44.

53. To be sure, it is entirely possible to oppose libertariansism from a religious point of view, provided only that this one element of religious belief be disregarded.

SIX   WEALTH AND WHIMSY: BEING RICH, PRODUCING RICHES

1. For a more thorough discussion, see Friedrich Hauck and Wilhelm Kasch, *Theological Dictionary of the New Testament* (Grand Rapids, Mich.: Eerdmans, 1976), 6:318–32.

2. The godfather of liberation theology is Gustavo Gutierrez; his *A Theology of Liberation* (New York: Orbis, 1973) remains the urtext of the vast literature produced by that movement. For a thorough critique of the movement, see Michael Novak, *Will It Liberate?* (New York: Paulist Press, 1986), and my theological evaluation in "Theology and Politics— A Cautionary Tale" in *The Catholic Moment* (Harper and Row, 1987).

3. Hauck and Kasch, *Theological Dictionary*, 6, p. 327.

4. Quoted in Michael Novak, *The Spirit of Democratic Capitalism* (New York: Simon and Schuster, 1982), p. 242. See also p. 397n, citing J. Philip Wogoman.

5. Eberhard Busch, *Karl Barth* (Philadelphia: Fortress, 1975), p. 382.

6. The quotations on economics are found in Karl Barth, *Church Dogmatics* III:4, pp. 525–53. The later statements regarding creativity and Mozart are in III:3, pp. 297ff.

7. Dietrich Bonhoeffer, *Ethics* (New York: Macmillan, 1955), pp. 209, 345.

8. Robert W. McElroy, *The Search for an American Public Theology* (New York: Paulist Press, 1989).

9. For the development of Niebuhr's economic thought, see Novak, *Spirit,* chap. 29.

10. Johan Huizinga, *Homo Ludens: A Study of the Play Element in Culture* (Boston: Beacon Press, 1955).

CONTRIBUTORS

PETER BERGER is director of the Institute for the Study of Economic Culture, Boston University. He is the author of many books, including *The Capitalist Revolution, Pyramids of Sacrifice,* and the classic *Invitation to Sociology.*

WALTER BLOCK is a senior research fellow at the Fraser Institute in Vancouver, British Colombia, and director of its Centre for the Study of Economics and Religion. He is the editor of fifteen books on economic and moral issues and has published numerous popular and scholarly articles on economics.

ROBERT GRANT is professor emeritus of religion, University of Chicago, and the author of *Early Christianity and Society.*

RICHARD JOHN NEUHAUS is director of the Institute on Religion and Public Life in New York City; has written a dozen books on religion, ethics, and public philosophy; and is editor-in-chief of *First Things: A Monthly Journal of Religion and Public Life.*

DAVID NOVAK is Edgar M. Bronfman Professor of Modern Judaic Studies at the University of Virginia. Novak is the author of six books, most recently *Jewish–Christian Dialogue: A Jewish Justification*, and numerous articles. An internationally known scholar of Jewish law and ethics, he has lectured extensively around the world and has served as a congregational rabbi for twenty-three years.

MICHAEL NOVAK holds the George Frederick Jewett Chair in Religion and Public Policy at the American Enterprise Institute in Washington, D.C., where he also serves as director of Social and Political Studies. Novak has written more than twenty books on philosophy, theology, politics, economics, and culture. He is also the author of more than two hundred articles, reviews, and essays published in popular journals including the *New Republic, Commentary, Harper's, Atlantic,* and *National Review.*

GEORGE WEIGEL is president of the Washington, D.C.–based Ethics and Public Policy Center. Weigel is the author of *Tranquillitas Ordinis: The Present Failure and Future Promise of American Catholic Thought on War and Peace* and *Catholicism and the Renewal of American Democracy.* His essays and reviews have appeared in the *Wall Street Journal, This World,* the *National Interest,* the *Washington Quarterly,* and numerous other periodicals.

THE CAPITALIST S·P·I·R·I·T

I s capitalism moral? The most productive generator of wealth the world has ever known, capitalism has made explosive economic growth and rising standards of living a reality for millions of people for the first time in history. At the same time, capitalism presents thorny ethical challenges for modern religious thought.

THE CAPITALIST SPIRIT represents the first search for a religious ethic of wealth creation. The authors explore the roots of anticapitalism in Judaism and Christianity, both of which tend to be concerned with the distribution of wealth rather than its creation. The book also considers the anticapitalist tendency of modern religious thinkers, including those who promote "liberation theology" in developing countries.

Edited by the renowned sociologist Peter L. Berger, THE CAPITALIST SPIRIT includes chapters by Michael Novak, George Weigel, Walter Block, Richard John Neuhaus, David Novak, and Robert Grant.